EQUALITY

Edited by

JANE FRANKLIN

Contents

Preface

Equality is a value or aspiration that continues to divide Left from Right in politics. Indeed, to the extent that those terms retain meaning they do so because of different attitudes to equality. Yet the differences are easier to sense than to make explicit. Everyone believes in the moral equality of human beings in some sense, though the sense is so vague as to have no practical implications whatever for many on the Right. Similarly, "equality before the law", is universally accepted, though nothing like it exists in the UK. This violation of a generally endorsed axiom arouses little indignation and few proposals for reform. Evidently society's revealed preference is for equality before the law – unless it is very expensive.

Beyond the more or less hollow support for those two principles of equality, the Right wants no further truck with the notion. It is the Left which wants to go further and therefore has to grapple with the idea and, in each generation, establish what equality means and what its current implications are. This book is an IPPR contribution to that exercise.

Its origin lies in a seminar and discussion group which has met irregularly at IPPR for a number of years. The group rejoiced in the sobriquet of the *Back to Basics* group until that title was adopted elsewhere for a less respectable initiative. The group was convened by James Cornford, the then-director of IPPR and Bhikhu Parekh, Professor of Political Theory at the University of Hull and an IPPR Trustee. It was concerned not so much to debate the philosophical foundations of socialism as to "occupy the elusive intermediate realm between philosophy and practice that can give us a critical purchase on contemporary reality without losing intimate touch with it". In other words, it sought to examine and clarify practical policy issues at their roots in values and ethical precepts. A latecomer to the group, I always found its deliberations unusually interesting and pertinent in cutting to the heart of many of the current ethical and political dilemmas facing the United Kingdom and modern societies in general.

This volume springs from papers written for the group on the theme of equality, one of the larger themes it has considered during its existence. In important respects it establishes reasonable and plausible objectives for the contemporary Left. I should like to thank James Cornford and Bhikhu Parekh for their seminal role in the group along with other regular participants: Brian Barry, G.A. Cohen, Caroline Daniel, John Dunn, Paul Hirst, David Miller, Onora O'Neill, Anne Phillips, Stuart White and Bernard Williams. Many of them have written chapters of the present volume but all are, to a greater or lesser extent, contributors.

Finally, I must thank Jane Franklin of the IPPR, who participated, acted as organiser for the group and who has ably edited this book.

The views and proposals published in this document are those of the authors. They are not necessarily endorsed by the IPPR, its staff or trustees.

Gerald Holtham

About the Contributors

Brian Barry is a Fellow of the British Academy and Professor of Political Science at the London School of Economics. He is currently engaged on a multi-volume Treatise on Social Justice of which the first two have been published: *Theories of Social Justice* (1989) and *Justice as Impartiality* (1975).

G A Cohen was educated at McGill and Oxford universities where he obtained, respectively, the degrees of BA in Philosophy and Politics and BPhil in Philosophy in 1963. For twenty-two years he was a Lecturer and then a Reader in Philosophy at University College, London. In 1985 he became Chichele Professor of Social and Political Theory and a Fellow of All Souls, Oxford. Professor Cohen is the author of *Karl Marx's Theory of History: A Defence* (1978), *History, Labour and Freedom* (1988), and *Self-Ownership, Freedom and Equality* (1995).

Caroline Daniel is a journalist at *The New Statesman*. Previously, she has been a journalist at *The Economist* and a researcher for Gordon Brown MP and was research editor for *Values, Visions and Voices* (1995), edited by Gordon Brown MP and Tony Wright MP. She read history at St John's College, Cambridge.

Jane Franklin is a Research Fellow at the Institute for Public Policy Research. Her main research interest is in the relationship between social and political theory, politics and policy making. She is currently editing *Politics of Risk Society*, Polity Press (1997) forthcoming, and an *IPPR/Polity Social Policy Reader*, also forthcoming.

David Miller is Official Fellow in Social Political Theory at Nuffield College, Oxford. His research interests include concepts of social justice, the ethics of markets and the ideas of nationality and citizenship. Among his books are *Market, State and Community* (Oxford, Clarendon Press, 1989), *On Nationality* (Oxford,

Clarendon Press, 1995), and with Michael Walzer, Pluralism, *Justice and Equality* (Oxford, Oxford University Press, 1995).

Professor Bhikhu Parekh is Professor of Political Theory at the University of Hull. He has been a Visiting Professor at many North American universities including Harvard where he was a Visiting Professor from January to June 1996. He has written extensively in the field of political philosophy and written and broadcast on race relations in Britain. His *Rethinking Multiculturalism* will be published this year by Macmillan.

Anne Phillips is Professor of Politics at London Guildhall University. Most of her writing deals with the relationship between socialism and feminism, but she currently works on issues of democracy and representation. Recent books include *Engendering Democracy* (Polity, 1991) and *The Politics of Presense* (OUP, 1995).

Dr Stuart White is an Assistant Professor in the Political Science Department, Massachusetts Institute of Technology. He was previously a Prize Research Fellow at Nuffield College, Oxford. His research interests concern the nature of egalitarian justice and the application of egalitarian ideals within the framework of advanced market economies. He is currently at work on a book-length manuscript, provisionally entitled, *The Civic Minimum: An Essay in the Political Theory of Social Citizenship.*

Bernard Williams was a member of the Commission on Social Justice. He has recently retired from the White's Professorship of Moral Philosophy at Oxford. He has also held chairs at London, Cambridge and Berkeley, and has been Provost of King's College, Cambridge. He was Chairman of the Home Office Committee on Obscenity and Film Censorship which reported in 1979.

Introduction
Jane Franklin

The idea of equality has become blurred and has lost its political appeal. Once the anchor of the politics of the Left, it seems to have slipped its traditional mooring and waits to be reconnected to the system of political ideals that guide politicians and policy makers. Often avoided as an uncomfortable idea which contains within it negative connotations of "levelling down" or "uniformity", its presence still haunts us as we witness the growing gap between rich and poor and the atrophy of the welfare state. Tony Blair has written that "liberty, equality and fraternity exist in creative tension. The fact the latter two have been ignored for too long means that the first is being increasingly denied. We need to redress the balance."[1] It is time to take a fresh look at equality.

Equality is a traditional idea. Tied to the two great ideologies of liberalism and socialism, its role as one of the guiding principles behind political, economic and social reform in this country has been firmly established over the course of the last two centuries. Like these systems of theory and practice, however, it is now open to question. There are two ways to respond to this. We can either argue that we have reached the "end of equality"[2] and that it no longer has a place in the language of politics, or we can say that we are at the beginning of a new way of seeing equality, and of building a new political language to take us into the future.

Any shift in the way we think about traditional ideas evokes a nostalgia for past associations as well as an excitement about future possibilities. But between these two responses, is a transitional phase of intense theoretical activity where we must take care to move with sensitivity and understanding, not to debunk traditional thinking but to engage with the transformation of ideas. While some on the Left despair at the abandonment of socialist tradition and others breathe a sigh of relief at the thought of jettisoning a principle which has become problematic, the ideas in this book will, I hope, generate a discussion of how the idea of equality in its many forms might infiltrate the political mind and influence the politics of the next century.

In our engagement with the idea of equality in these pages, you will find no single definition, no central theory of application, but a multiplicity of approaches, which bring the idea alive and shape its potential. Our authors inquire into the nature of equality: whether or not it is a timeless idea which exists independently of political intervention and how far it can bend to political expediency. They describe the fluidity of the idea as it shifts from the economic, to the political, to the social sphere and how it relates to the idea of community. They assess the strength of the idea, whether or not strict or diluted equality is appropriate to any given situation. They ask how we occupy that elusive space between ideas and politics and which takes priority over the other.

They offer an evaluation and critique of the philosophical foundations of the Commission on Social Justice, an independent inquiry into social and economic reform in the UK, set up at the instigation of the late Rt Hon John Smith QC MP, in 1992. The Commission sets out the philosophical framework for its inquiry in *The Justice Gap* (1993), taking *social justice* as its defining principle and recognising that social justice has "something to do with equality". The question then arises, "equality of what?"[3] The Commission answers this question as it sets out its four principles of social justice:

- The foundation of a free society is the equal worth of all its citizens
- Everyone is entitled, as a right of citizenship, to be able to meet their basic needs
- The right to self-respect and personal autonomy demands the widest possible spread of opportunities
- Not all inequalities are unjust, but unjust inequalities should be reduced and where possible eliminated.[4]

The key to understanding how the idea of equality operates within this framework, and indeed throughout this book, is to link it with the concepts that bring it into focus. In *The Justice Gap*, it is initially linked with status, making the active, legitimising force for equality a just society; secondly it is linked with citizenship and a political definition of basic needs; thirdly with freedom and opportunity; and fourthly with justice, which renders certain inequalities just.

The choice as to which concepts frame definitions of equality, is in turn linked to political, ideological and religious values. Caroline Daniel looks at the fate of equality over the past century to see how its dimensions have altered and adapted to changing circumstances. At the beginning of the century, we can observe how it is attached to the socialist critique of poverty and becomes a force for the redistribution of material resources. By the 1950s, as Britain becomes a more affluent society, it shifts to the social sphere, supported by the idea of social justice and promoted as "equality of opportunity". By the 1970s, this optimism for a socially just meritocracy was undermined by the growing economic crisis. The idea then moves away from its attachment to class, status and wealth, towards the relationship between particular groups and individuals in society, as in the campaigns for racial and sexual equality, and takes on the mantle of liberation. Then the relationship of equality to freedom changes. In the 1980s, the very concept of society is challenged and the idea of equality is lost to the idea of freedom. Those on the Left who still believed that equality is an essential concept of socialist politics, endeavoured to accommodate the idea of individual liberty with the idea of equality. So much so, some have argued, that it has lost its radical edge.

G A Cohen argues that this accommodation of values, as articulated in the philosophical framework of the Commission on Social Justice, undermines the firm foundation of values that the Labour party needs if it is to have any moral force or political character. Contrary to the views of the Commission, he argues, the values of community and equality are not conditional on changing circumstance and do not need to be adapted to take account of social, economic or political reality. For Cohen, these values are always there, to give social movements and political actors a goal and a focus for change. They represent a vision which need not correspond with reality, but motivates change toward that vision. Cohen defines the principle of equality in material terms: "the measure of amenity and burden in one person's life should be roughly comparable to that in any other's". He argues that the

Commission abandons equality as a principle in these terms when it asserts that "inequalities are not necessarily unjust but unjustified inequalities should be reduced and where possible eliminated" and that "redistribution of income is a means to social justice and not an end in itself". The ideal of community represents a particular mode of human relationships says Cohen, and complete rejection of the logic of the market. In fact, community is *anti*-market because the market inspires production, not on the basis of commitment to one's fellow human beings and a desire to serve them while being served by them, but on the basis of impersonal cash reward. The socialist aspiration is therefore to extend community to the whole of our economic life. The Commission does not, Cohen argues, invoke community as a core value in these terms.

Without a firm, moral foundation, Labour has to construct a new identity and in doing so becomes indistinguishable from the Liberal Democrats. Cohen argues that "no Liberal or Tory could object" to the Commission's four principles of social justice and that "to modify principles for the sake of electoral gain can be electorally counter-productive". In undermining the principles which people have always associated with the Labour party, the Commission runs the risk of contributing to electoral failure.

Bernard Williams, a member of the Commission on Social Justice, addresses the complex relationship between principle and electoral success. He agrees with Cohen that principles provide a firm foundation for the Left, but argues that we cannot take traditional principles for granted: they are not immutable, and to understand them we need to inquire as to the circumstances which generated their appeal and understand the particular historical conditions in which they were deployed. Unless we trace this relationship between tradition and the changing world we live in, we will lose touch with both. The Commission acknowledges that, at the time of the Beveridge Report in 1945, there was perhaps a special feeling of class solidarity and a sense of national community which grew out of the experience of the Second World War. But this has changed, and many people now have a more individualised identity, and cannot accept principles which are out of step with the way they live their lives. For the Left to generate political support, it is necessary to question traditional principles and move beyond a nostalgic attachment to beliefs that no longer resonate with the electorate. This does not mean that we have to reject them out of hand, but that we should engage with them to explore their relevance for present circumstances. In this context, Williams disputes the charge that the Commission disparages equality, rather, he suggests, it raises questions about what equality *is* and what it should be equality *of*. All ideas and theoretical assumptions should be open to interpretation and their traditional status does not exempt them from scrutiny. In fact, the radicalism of the principles of social justice and equality does not arise from principles themselves but in their potential *effect*. As a *political* idea, equality must be open to interpretation, which legitimately takes place in the context of other competing political values. The nature of this interpretation will affect the outcome.

Stuart White places the values of equality and social justice side by side and inquires into what those who believe in equality want and whether the strategy of the Commission on Social Justice can provide the institutional means to deliver it. White suggests that egalitarians should want a society which satisfies the principles of an "egalitarian perspective on social justice". These include the *brute luck principle* (which requires that we correct for or prevent disadvantage attributable to differential "brute luck"); the *fair exchange principle* (which requires that we protect individuals from excessive vulnerability in the market-place, and its potentially exploitative effects); and the *reciprocity principle* (which requires that we prevent economic free-riding). In *The Justice Gap*, the Commission explicitly rejects the brute luck principle, at least in its simplest and strongest form. Nevertheless, White argues that the Commission's strategy of "endowment egalitarianism" underpinned by an active welfare state, is an ethically attractive one from the standpoint of the remaining principles of egalitarian justice, though his support is subject to qualification. White contends that in setting out its strategy, the Commission exaggerates the interdependency between justice and efficiency, and understates the extent to which a strategy for achieving social justice must inevitably rely upon conventional income redistribution. In addition, whilst the Commission tacitly endorses the reciprocity principle, it fails rigorously to pursue some of the "tougher" implications of this principle in the areas of welfare policy and the tax treatment of inheritance. In conclusion, White considers that there is much that the egalitarian can and should welcome in the Commission's report, but calls for further development of the Commission's reform strategy, and of its philosophical foundations.

David Miller turns our attention to the *kind* of equality the Left should pursue. He suggests that much of the debate about equality has been skewed towards material equality and arguments for equality of outcome or equality of opportunity – whether all have an equal share of resources or all have an equal opportunity to strive for unequal resources. Miller puts forward a persuasive argument for a third alternative and a way forward for the Left – *social equality or equality of status*: "when each member of a society regards herself as fundamentally the equal of all the others and is regarded by the others as fundamentally their equal." In such a society, there would be no hierarchical barriers to friendship and solidarity. It would, in effect, be a classless society in which social equality stands alongside equality of opportunity to "correct its elitist tendencies". This option, he argues, will appeal to many who wish to open up relationships between individuals so that they can relate to each directly without the inhibition of status difference.

Miller disagrees with Cohen in that he believes that it is not equality *per se* that distinguishes socialists from other political viewpoints, but the emphasis and significance given to equality by those on the Left. It is not, he argues, that socialists believe in equality while the others do not, but "that they give equality a higher priority, or have a better grasp of what it actually takes to implement a principle like equality of opportunity". Miller argues that real material equality is beyond the grasp of market economies and is, in many cases unjust. If those on the Left could accept this, they could move forward and work towards a form of equality that is distinctive and achievable. It is an attractive proposition that would appeal to many who wish to overcome the divisions of a class-based society and one that attaches itself to the more individualised identities of the 1990s.

Anne Phillips takes us further into the intricacies of the meaning of equality, contrasting the arguments for equality between men and women in both the liberal and socialist traditions. Socialists have argued that women have been constrained by their domestic role in the family, while liberals tend to defend the private family from public intervention and are much less likely to regard the household as a place of confinement. Phillips explains how "difference between the two traditions has sometimes been theorised as a difference between pursuing equality of opportunities and achieving equality of outcomes: liberalism typically focusing on removing the *legal* constraints to free up equality of opportunities; socialism typically addressing the *structural* conditions that are necessary to substantial equality". She traces the evolution of the debate between the two theoretical traditions through to the 1990s, where, she argues, feminists still focus on the double burden of women who have to juggle home and work responsibilities. This persistent association between women and care work underlies all sexual inequalities in the labour market and Phillips sees no way out of this short of equalising care work between women and men. Such an outcome requires strict equality between the sexes. Can socialism help to bring this about? There has been a distinctive feminisation of Left politics during the 1990s, not least in the recruitment of women as political representatives, with increasing attention being paid to the double burden of women. Yet, this may owe more, Phillips contends, to the recent convergence between liberal and socialist values than to anything specific to the socialist tradition. Socialist ideas can, however, offer a scale of values radically different from that which shores up an unregulated market economy. Socialist values can provide the impetus for a social democratic regulation of the market, so that "production is tailored to social need and caring for people takes equal priority alongside producing marketable goods and services". This implies that unless we separate out the inequalities and differences which are attached to the accident of being born male or female from individual differences we might otherwise accept, we shall never achieve equality between men and women. In arguing this, socialism may take its cue from liberalism, but it may have a stronger political will to make it happen.

In *Equality in a Multicultural Society*, Bhikhu Parekh considers how we might construct a culturally sensitive theory of equality.

He examines the real dilemmas that different cultures and societies have faced and the ways in which they have endeavoured to resolve them, drawing out some of the general theoretical implications. Parekh shows us how the discussion of equality in Western political thought has largely ignored the importance of culture, taking an homogeneous society for granted. This lack of cultural sensitivity has meant, that although political thinkers have discussed legal, civil, political and other rights of citizens, they have rarely touched on the question of cultural rights, either as the individual's right *to* culture or as the rights *of* cultures or cultural communities. They have asked whether, why and within what limits all human beings or citizens should be treated equally, but have not raised these questions in relation to cultures. If we interpret human beings and their actions, choices, preferences in terms of the systems of meaning characteristic of their cultures we have greater opportunity to do them justice.

As Parekh has argued elsewhere,[5] almost every modern state is characterised by cultural diversity, but is faced with the questions of how to accommodate differences without losing social cohesion, how to reconcile the apparently conflicting demands of equality of treatment and recognition of cultural differences, and how to create a spirit of common citizenship among its culturally diverse members. If we are to ensure fairness and equality in culturally diverse societies, we need to do two things. First, we must appreciate that equal treatment might have to be different and not identical in its content. Second, we need to develop appropriate conceptual and institutional tools to ensure that different treatment does not lead to unfair discrimination or privilege.

Given the diversity of opinion, even among those who aim to embody broadly egalitarian ideals in practical politics, can policy makers on the Left make any "practical, real-world choices that decrease inequality."[6] Brian Barry sets out to leap over what he sees as the short term electoral consensus of policy makers and politicians, to propose changes in the nature of economic and social relations which will have a real impact in creating a more equal society. He presents the case for a single measure which would, when fully implemented, make a significant difference to the quality of people's lives. This measure is basic income. His plea for a radical, practical approach to thinking about equality is an example of a far reaching idea for which a political consensus would *have* to be built. Barry is critical of the "narrow conception of the constraints of political feasibility" in the report of the Commission on Social Justice and asserts "that those who drafted the report were reduced to cobbling together proposals originating from the various pressure groups associated with different members of the Commission". While it is crucial to think radically, to drive the political will forward, the Commission was concerned to balance radical ideas with politically viable ones. They considered the idea of basic income and set out their proposals for "participation income", which, they suggested, would operate as a way of modernising the social insurance system by placing a higher value on some types of unpaid work, thereby leaving the door open for basic, or citizen's income.[7]

Barry is critical of this gradual approach and of the negative responses with which the idea of basic income is often met. He asks why such an essentially simple idea has failed to make the breakthrough into mainstream political discourse. There has, he contends, been a great tendency in the literature to down play the radical potential of basic income. It offers a genuinely new deal – a different way of relating individual and society. Compatible with the ideas of such socialist thinkers as William Morris and R H Tawney, it not only limits disparities in income but also gives each person the dignity that comes from independence and is a practical way of achieving some of their central aims. Indeed, Barry argues that if we can manage to strip away the appalling legacy of "actually existing socialism" and go back to Marx's original utopian vision, it is not absurd to suggest that a subsistence-level basic income is a far more plausible institutional embodiment of it than anything Marx himself ever came up with. This is an idea waiting in the wings, and is worth taking seriously, Barry argues, as a way forward for the Left.

As Cohen tells us, the relationship between theory and practice is complex. Ideas provide the backdrop to political activity, a reference point, a rallying cry. There is a passion in the idea of equality that will not go away. Nelson Mandela came to Britain in the Summer of 1996 and had an extraordinary effect on the people who saw and heard him. He inspired the feeling among ordinary people and politicians alike, that we are all equal, all the same, that before we are men and women, black and white, catholic and protestant, we are human beings and we can change the world we live in. As we enter the twenty-first century, and globalisation and technological change transform all our lives, we are at risk of marginalising a substantial number of people who are unable to participate in this transformation. The practice of "actually existing socialism" as Barry has pointed out, has been discredited. But there is still a hunger for a more equal and just society which drives us to search for new political forms to achieve that end. The language of this new politics may at first be unfamiliar. It may be structured more by time, space and access to information rather than by status, wealth or opportunity. Who knows? In this book, we have taken one step towards the revitalising an idea that may inspire a new generation.

Endnotes

1. T Blair "Ideological Blurring", *Prospect,* June 1996.

2. M Kaus (1992) *The End of Equality,* New York, Basic Books.

3. *The Justice Gap* IPPR (1993) p7.

4. *The Justice Gap,* IPPR (1993).

5. B Parekh (1994) "Equality, Fairness and Limits of Cultural Diversity" in *Innovation,* Vol 7, No 3.

6. Henry Milner quoted in Brian Barry "The Attractions of Basic Income", p157.

7. See *Social Justice: Strategies for National Renewal,* The Report of the Commission on Social Justice pp 261-265.

SOCIALISTS AND EQUALITY
Caroline Daniel

Egalitarianism has been a key theme of British socialism for much of this century. George Bernard Shaw opened with his idealistic advocacy of equality of income. R H Tawney followed on with a vision of a society brought together in fellowship by greater equality. Then came Anthony Crosland's hope of social equality and Hugh Gaitskell's admission, in 1955, that "the central socialist ideal is equality".[1] In the 1960s, the focus of debate shifted towards the more distinct areas of racial and sexual inequality, but by the 1980s, there had been a further change. Margaret Drabble, writing in 1988, observed that "twenty years ago, a profession of faith in egalitarianism was not considered improper or eccentric. It is now. By some shift of usage, by some change in the climate of thought, egalitarianism has become a dirty word, a devalued word".[2] Politicians on the left today are certainly squeamish about the little word "equality". In this paper I shall trace the development of the concept of equality over the last hundred years, how it evolves and adapts to political necessity and how it is debated as an idea and as a political tool.

The problem is that although most people want equality of something, there is no consensus about what should be equalised. As Crosland put it in *Socialism Now*, "what are the main causes of inequality – inherited wealth, inherited IQ, home circumstances, hard work or luck? What are the most important inequalities? Are they of income, capital, education, housing or industrial power? Or are they between the sexes or between races? Or are they perhaps of privacy, sunlight and access to unpolluted beaches?"[3] Different interpretations of equality can conflict. Equality of opportunity may conflict with equality of outcome; equality of income with equality of respect. As David Miller has argued, "The conflict is not about the value of equality as such, but about competing specifications of that value, about different versions of what it means to treat people as equals".[4] Tawney's egalitarianism, for example, arises from his

Christian belief that we are all equal before God; Bentham assumed the existence of equal passions; and J S Mill equal rationality. Robert Burns expressed many a socialist's view that "A man's a man for a' that" and G D H Cole echoed that "socialism is an imaginative belief that all men, however unequal we may be in powers of mind and body, or in capacity for service, are in a really significant sense equal, not merely before the law but one with another". Raymond Williams in *Culture and Society* (1958) thought that "the only inequality that is evil is inequality that denies the essential equality of being". And Douglas Jay asked in *Socialism and the New Society* (1962):

> why should I have more right to happiness than you? ... if we believe that all human beings have an equal right to happiness and a civilised life, then it is for this reason that we should seek to establish a society in which these rights are embodied. The ultimate ground for condemning inequality is that it is unjust, not that it causes resentment or envy.

This belief is still evocative today. "The foundation of a free society is the equal worth of its citizens",[5] was the first of the four core principles of the Commission on Social Justice. But how far does equal worth take us in practice?

The Fabians and meeting basic needs

The early Fabians, who were united by their criticism of poverty, argued for a national minimum standard of living, and state regulation of the economy and state provision of free services to provide the background conditions for equal access to the market. Amy Gutmann, in *Liberal Equality*, noted that "the idea of equality served a critical purpose for most early Fabians – as a critique of a society that denied the effective opportunity for all citizens to live decently".[6] The compassionate desire to ensure that everyone has their basic needs met is reflected in the second core principle of the Commission on Social Justice, "everyone is entitled, as a right of citizenship, to be able to meet their basic needs".[7]

The Fabians developed the concept of economic surplus to justify their attack on social privilege. As Geoffrey Foote explains, "they believed that the wages of the workers were determined by the demand for their different skills. Any wages above a subsistence level were seen as a form of rent of ability ... however, in capitalist society a large proportion of the workers' rent was directed into the pockets of the private owners and preserved for the children of the capitalists".[8] The Fabians wanted to see this surplus used for the benefit of all. They argued that the marginal utility of income and wealth progressively diminishes, so that the satisfaction of the basic needs of the poor should have priority over the desires of the rich.

George Bernard Shaw and equality of income

George Bernard Shaw took a more radical position and called for equality of income, "unless we can see the expediency of this, we are not socialists: we are only pitiers of the poor and rebels against unpleasantness".[9] Shaw argued that capitalism was both unjust and inefficient since it involved a misdirection of production, producing "frippery and luxury whilst the nation is rotting for want of good food".[10] He assessed seven different methods of distributing money to see if any of them could provide an alternative to the present system: "to each what she produces", to "each what she deserves", "to each what she can grab", "to the common people enough to keep them alive whilst they work all day, and the rest to the gentry", "distribution by class", "let us go on as we are", and "socialism: an equal share to everybody".[11] The only solution, Shaw concluded was to give everyone the same. He imagined a system in which material incentives would be replaced by a sense of public duty, although he accepted that coercion might be needed to get people to work. He hoped that equality of income would promote a true meritocracy, for between "persons of equal income there is no social distinction except the distinction of merit. Money is nothing: character, conduct and capacity are everything".[12]

Equality and poverty

For the early Fabians, the alleviation of poverty was the prime motivation for the redistribution of wealth. As Anthony Crosland put it, "at any time up to 1939, the case for greater equality, at least of incomes, seemed self-evident. By making the rich less rich the poor could be made less poor ... to take some caviar from the rich and distribute it in bread to the poor, was a clear moral imperative".[13] But can this be taken to mean that arguments for equality are not really about any desire for equality, but just for levelling everyone up to a basic minimum? Joseph Raz has argued that:

> what makes us care about various inequalities is not the inequality, but the concern identified with the underlying principle. It is the hunger of the hungry, the need of the needy ... the fact that they are worse off in the relevant respect than their neighbour is relevant. But it is relevant not as an independent evil of inequality. Its relevance is in showing that their hunger is greater, their need more pressing, their suffering more hurtful and therefore it is our concern for the hungry, the needy, the suffering and not our concern for equality that makes us give them priority.[14]

This perspective can be used to criticise some of the early Fabian arguments for redistribution. However both Richard Tawney and Anthony Crosland show that there are reasons for equality that go beyond just the satisfaction of basic needs.

Tawney and Community

In *Equality* (1931) Tawney worked out a comprehensive theory of equality. He appealed to the Christian ideal that we are all equal before God and endorsed the Fabian position which asserted the need to guarantee each citizen a decent life, but went further. His real concern was to build a common culture and a sense of community. Equality was a means to secure fellowship. The inequality he deplored was not "inequality of personal gifts, but of the social and economic environment ... not with a biological phenomenon, but with the spiritual relation and conduct based on it".[15] The solution for Tawney lay in the realm of ideas and principles. He rejected the Webb's focus on changing institutional arrangements. His politics was one characterised by moral vexation not economic amelioration. To change, society needed to "destroy the moral, social, economic and historical credentials of the *status quo*", and discredit the acquisitive culture. He wanted to replace the culture of competition with one based on co-operation and fellowship, where people saw themselves as equal citizens. A society that valued equality would place more significance on the differences of character and intelligence between individuals, and a low degree of significance on social or economic differences. Tawney condemned the "habit of mind which thinks it, not regrettable, but natural and desirable, that different sections of the community should be distinguished from one another by sharp differences of economic status, of environment, of education and culture and habit of life".[16]

Tawney did not call for exact equality of income, but equality of "environment, habits of life, of access to education and the means of civilisation, of security and independence, and of the social considerations which equality in these matters usually carries with it". He accepted that people were unequal in natural endowments, or in the capacity to develop them by education.

To criticise inequality and to desire equality is not, as is sometimes suggested, to cherish the romantic illusion that men are equal in character and intelligence. It is to hold that while natural endowments may differ profoundly, it is the mark of a civilised society to aim at eliminating such inequalities as have their source, not in individual differences, but in its own organisation.[17]

Tawney thought that some measure of income inequality was justifiable since "inequality of circumstance is regarded as reasonable, in so far as it is the necessary condition of securing the services which the community requires ... when a reasonable provision has been made for all, exceptional responsibilities should be compensated by exceptional rewards, as a recognition of the service performed and an inducement to perform it".[18] These intuitions were later developed by Anthony Crosland and John Rawls. Inequalities could be justified if they were to the benefit of the worst off.

Tawney did not favour an equal opportunity society. He accepted that privileged positions should be won on merit, believing that "individual happiness does not only require that men should be free to rise to new positions of comfort and distinction; it also requires that they should be able to lead a life of dignity and culture, whether they rise or not".[19] Tawney showed that there were reasons for redistribution that went beyond the alleviation of absolute poverty, and that there were reasons to limit the advantages of those at the top, as well as provide for those at the bottom. Tawney recognised that in accepting individual difference, a hierarchy of birth could be replaced with a hierarchy of talent.

Anthony Crosland and Social Equality

Writing in the post austerity years of the 1950s, Crosland was keen to distance himself from the dour values of the Webb's in their call for hard work, self-discipline, efficiency, research and abstinence. His was a liberating, expansive socialism. In *The Future of Socialism*, his paean to social equality, he called for "liberty and gaiety in private life: the need for a reaction against the Fabian tradition". Britain needed not only higher exports and old age pensions but more open air cafés, brighter and "gayer streets at night, later closing hours for public houses, more local repertory theatres ... and so on ad infinitum"[20]. Socialism and affluence could go hand in hand.

Crosland emphasised social, rather than material, equality. He believed that economic growth, full employment and improvements in the welfare state had reduced the need for further redistribution of wealth, while social inequalities still created collective resentments, evident in strikes and social unrest, which could undermine democracy, social and industrial peace, tolerance and freedom. Secondly, Crosland argued for greater equality on the grounds of social justice. It was unjust, he argued to pay for an education which would provide overwhelming social privilege; it was unjust to inherit wealth since it could be gained without merit, carried no corresponding obligation, and not everyone had an equal opportunity to acquire it; and rewards from work could be unjust, because they were sometimes linked to nepotism, and the old school tie. Thirdly, he believed that social inequality was wasteful and inefficient, it stood in the way of social mobility and prevented genuine equality of opportunity. A society based on equal of opportunity, provided it was genuinely fair, would prevent the top rewards being reserved for a pre-selected few, would encourage mobility and would be efficient in selecting people on merit for top jobs.

Is equality of opportunity enough?

Although Crosland is frequently seen as the chief proponent of equality of opportunity, his support was qualified. Many of the reasons behind his doubts find an echo in the views of John Rawls, set out in *A Theory of Justice*.[21] In *Socialism Now*, Crosland openly linked his views to those of Rawls, when he claimed that he adopted "the strong definition of equality – what Rawls has subsequently called the "democratic" as opposed to the liberal conception of equality of opportunity".[22] The liberal conception of equality of opportunity (sometimes called the minimalist interpretation) is mainly concerned with the progressive removal of legal impediments to recruitment, and giving all children a fair start in schools. It is a procedural notion, concerned with making sure that the race for positions, or unequal outcomes, is a fair one. For Crosland, this did not fulfil the requirements of social justice. An equal opportunity society is more than a meritocratic society in which the greatest rewards go to those with the most fortunate family background. Raymond Plant summed up his view: "Crosland had a belief in equality, with inequalities being justified if, and only if, differential rewards work to the benefit of the community as a whole and we can assume that access to jobs which command differential rewards would be on the basis of genuine equality of opportunity".[23] This is very close to John Rawls' principles of justice: "Each person to have the most extensive system of equal basic liberties compatible with similar liberties for all", and "social and economic inequalities to be arranged so that they are (a) to the greatest advantage to the least advantaged consistent with a just savings principle, and (b) attached to offices and positions open to all under conditions of fair equality of opportunity".[24]

But there are clear differences between the two approaches. Crosland thought his instinctive view of social justice "not susceptible to proof or disproof". He therefore relied on the "moral predilections of the reader". Rawls' theory was needed to "round out Crosland's intellectual position", according to Plant. Rawls wanted to get away from this subjective approach. Keen to link ordinary moral feelings to an objective case for equality, Rawls adopted the idea of a social contract in which he imagined individuals living in a state of ignorance of their own talents and abilities. From behind this veil of ignorance, individuals could make objective choices as to the principles which should govern social life. However, Crosland grappled with a feeling that egalitarianism was not a consensus value. How was it possible to move towards an egalitarian principle of distribution when people both know their talents, and want to keep the rewards they can earn from them?

After Crosland

By the 1970s, Crosland's optimism had fizzled out, as the growing economic crisis undermined his more comprehensive ambitions. Incomes were not naturally growing closer together and low growth made plans for painless redistribution redundant. Arguments for social equality gave way to arguments for sexual and racial equality. The call for equal opportunities for women, for example, was pushed higher up the political agenda, resulting in the 1970 Equal Pay Act and the 1975 Sex Discrimination Act.

Interpretations as to the sources of inequality also changed at this time. Nick Bosanquet argued that:

We now see poverty more in relative than absolute terms, but our view of the sources of inequality have also changed. We have come to fear the effects of the tax and social security system on inequality ... we have also become much less optimistic about whether the educational system can ever contribute very much to equality. The government was thus faced with the challenge of inequality arising from the old natural sources and also with a greater challenge of finding a more equitable way of financing public spending. The redistributive effects of public spending might well be undermined by the increasingly regressive way in which it was financed.[25]

The forces that created inequalities in the first place, and which perpetuated them, were too strong to be resisted through indirect methods. Inequalities had to be tackled at their source, through more equal incomes, attacking the culture of inequality. John Goldthorpe argued that the only way to create a more equal society was through collective action by the working classes. Piecemeal measures misjudged the resistance of the class structure to attempts to change it.[26]

Equality and liberty

But the climate for equality was changing, and these views were challenged by those who sensed that equality now had to come to terms with freedom. For Raymond Plant equality was "the distinctive socialist value", nevertheless his main priority was to make equality compatible with liberty. "It is because we value liberty for all, that we are concerned to secure a greater equality in the worth of liberty" arguing that a fair distribution of the worth of liberty is "going to involve far greater equality of income and wealth as well as the provision of services", because differences of income lead to differences in the use of other sorts of basic welfare goods. Plant's conclusion is blunt. "Except in conditions of high economic growth the greater equality in the worth of liberty cannot be attained without a certain amount of levelling down. We have to be clear about this".[27]

But the political context did not prove amenable to such thinking. "The current political and intellectual climate is deeply hostile to egalitarian ideas", observed Plant.[28] Doubts about the role of public spending combined with a resurgence in new right thinking summed up by Keith Joseph and Jonathan Sumption in *Equality* (1979) when they argue that equality of opportunity "requires that no external barrier shall prevent an individual from exploiting his talents. No laws shall permit some men to do what is forbidden by others". They do not admit that equality of dignity or self-respect has anything to do with equality of wealth. Freedom lay in the absence of coercion, not the absence of cash, or as they famously put it "poverty is not unfreedom". They called Tawney's hopes of changing man's competitive instincts "despotic". Inequality was merely "a state of affairs which results when the natural aptitudes of men are allowed to manifest themselves in natural differences". People do not have the same earning power. Income was paid not according to desert, or merit, but according to the value of work to others. They concluded that the best way to help the poor was not through redistribution, but through trickle-down: "you can only make the poor better off by making everyone richer, including the rich".[29]

These criticisms hit home and supporters of equality were anxious to show that equality was not incompatible with freedom. In 1986, Neil Kinnock wrote in *The Future of Socialism* that Labour had allowed itself to assume that liberty was not important, "efficiency, individual liberty, wealth creation, patriotism; such a vocabulary is thought to be unfamiliar to the Labour movement ... the objective past, present and future of democratic socialism is individual freedom. And the means which democratic socialism has chosen to protect that freedom are equality and democracy". Rather than look to growth as the means to effect redistribution, Kinnock wanted to create a strong body of moral opinion in favour of equality. "Political economy is not ultimately a question of economic organisation or historical inevitability, but moral choice".[30] Roy Hattersley agreed. His book *Choose Freedom*[31] was a clear attempt to paint Labour as the party of freedom, with equality playing a leading role.

Equality, justice and efficiency

The other criticism that had hit home was that equality was incompatible with efficiency. The emphasis by Le Grand and the others on the need for direct attacks on money inequality seemed to interfere with the workings of the free market, and paid insufficient regard to the fact that some of the inequalities the market generated could be seen as just. Rather than argue the "moral" case for equality, more pragmatic thinkers have tried to move with the spirit of the neo-liberal times, by framing their case for equality in the language of economic efficiency.

The Justice Gap also tries to meld equality with efficiency. It does not accept that all inequalities are unjust. The paper can be read as an attempt to move away from Rawlsian thinking, and liberal egalitarianism more generally, by invoking the concepts of entitlement and desert.

> It seems fair, for instance, that a medical student should receive a lower income than the fully qualified doctor; or that experience or outstanding talent should be rewarded ... most people believe that it is fair for people to bequeath their property as they see fit, even though this means that some will inherit more than others ... parents can, however, pass on intelligence, talent, charm and other qualities, as well as property or titles. Rawls in his theory rests a lot on the fact that a person's talents, and his or her capacity to make productive use of those talents, are very much matters of luck and are also, in some part, the product of society. Nobody, he has rightly insisted, *deserves* his or her natural talents ... but Rawls's argument applies as much to effort as to raw talent ... virtually everything about a person that yields a product is itself undeserved. So no rewards, on Rawls's view, are at the most basic level a matter of desert. Few people believe this... As the American philosopher Robert Nozick forcefully put it, why does "desert have to go all the way down?[32]

Ronald Dworkin's arguments are relevant to this critique of Rawls. In Dworkin's terms, the goal of equality of income is insufficiently "ambition sensitive" as well as insufficiently "endowment sensitive". Income equality does not permit income inequality where this results not from differences in productive capacity over which the individuals have no control, or which are matters of brute luck, but from different choices persons make as how to deploy their productive capacities. But if you or I have the same opportunity to earn a certain amount, but I choose not to make use of the opportunity to earn a certain amount, while you take it, is the ensuing income inequality really unjust? What *The Justice Gap* report attempts to do is restore some role for individual ambition, or effort.

It is easy to see that the role of choice does affect the way we view the justice of different distributions. We need information about how the inequalities have come about before we can decide if a particular distribution is fair or unfair. So if A earns more money than B because A works harder, this seems fairer than if A earns more money that B (for the same job) because B is discriminated against by a racially prejudiced employer. So, for example, it seems fair that someone who smokes should pay more for their insurance because of the extra risk they know they are taking on by smoking. Yet it may seem unfair that someone gets turned down for insurance because of factors beyond their control, such as inheriting certain genes. If the outcome is the result of individual choice then it seems fair. As Dworkin says "people's fate should depend on their ambitions but should not depend on their natural and social endowments". When inequalities of income are created by choices not circumstances Rawls' difference principle would create not remove unfairness.

Yet there may be a situation where trying to be distribution sensitive will conflict with ambition sensitivity. Some people will be unreservedly disadvantaged by circumstances beyond their control, such as being handicapped. However, showing equal concern for advantaged and disadvantaged requires something other than maximal redistribution to the disadvantaged. The disadvantaged can never be fully compensated for their unequal endowments as this would involve some kind of slavery of the advantaged.

Between equality of opportunity and equality of outcome

Distinctions between equality of opportunity and equality of outcome continue to shape the debate about equality. It helps to look at equality of opportunity in a linear way. At the beginning you have a fair start, and at the end there are winners and losers. The idea of the fair start is that there should be no legal barriers preventing anyone from taking part. So, the fact that a tiny number of women, or black people, do not succeed in becoming doctors, does not mean that the race is unfairly run.

As we have already seen, socialists have typically questioned this. The absence of legal barriers is not enough to ensure that the race is a fair one. Some may start with an economic handicap, which prevents them from making the most of opportunities on offer. The way to address this is to ensure that people's minimum needs are met, hence the Webb's advocacy of a national minimum standard of living, and Tawney's call for a basic level of practical equality. At issue is the question as to how far it is practical to intervene to make the start fair. And, if the start cannot be made fair, how far should the outcomes be interfered with?

This can be illustrated by the debate between Roy Hattersley and Gordon Brown. Hattersley argues that:

> I certainly want equality of outcome ... many inequalities are not the result of genetics, even less of fate. They are the product of the way in which society is organised ... socialists want first to reduce and then eliminate the organisational, institutional and social factors which make men and women unnaturally different.

For Hattersley, equality of outcome is "the belief that those who fall behind in the race should not be told that they had their chance and failed but should be given a new impetus to run on.[33]

Gordon Brown sees things differently: "the essence of equality is equality of opportunity".[34] He develops a dynamic, progressive model of equality of opportunity, where there is not just one race, but several, so if you fall at the first hurdle, this will not automatically disadvantage you for the rest of the race. He clearly takes Dworkin's view that there are limits to how far it is possible to compensate those who start the race unequally. And that some inequalities can be justified by a degree of effort and desert. He proposes a politics of second chances. Like the Commission on Social Justice, he is keen to dispel fears that there is a trade-off between equality and efficiency. Inequality, Brown argues, "affects us all because whether it is in high social security bills and high taxes or in the waste of economic potential, every one of us pays a heavy price as a result". Equality of opportunity, he argues secures a more equal society and is also the key to economic prosperity.

Conclusion

The current academic and political climate has come a long way from the ambitions of George Bernard Shaw, and even those set out in Labour's 1974 Manifesto which called for "a fundamental and irreversible shift in the balance of power and wealth in favour of working people and their families ... far greater economic equality – in income, wealth and living standards ... and an increase in social equality by giving far greater importance to full employment, housing, education and social benefits".

It is an illustration of how attitudes to equality have changed that this declaration seems absurdly extreme. Now money redistribution is politically taboo. Arguments about equality have evolved to fit changed political and economic circumstances. Crosland's thinking can be understood in terms of his desire to find a way beyond nationalisation, and accept a wider role for the market. He was also conscious of the dilemma of how to get people to vote for redistribution, when it was against their fiscal self-interest. His answer lay in growth. But when this failed, egalitarianism fell apart. Similarly Brown is conscious of the fact that talking of equality of outcome, as Hattersley does, would be political suicide. Yet the phrase "equality of opportunity" is the rhetorical equivalent of elevator music. Rather bland and meaningless. The language of "fairness" has more salience with today's electorate than "equality", which many still equate with higher taxation.

Money redistribution is becoming less central to academic debate too. Michael Walzer, for example, chooses to stress not money equality, but complex equality. This recognises that there are a number of different dimensions along which individuals can be scored, but does not mean that the scores should be equalised within one particular dimension. Overall equality can be attained by balancing out the inequalities that emerge in different spheres, and ensuring that goods are distributed according to appropriate criteria. So health care should not be distributed solely on the basis of cash considerations. Political power should likewise not be abused to gain access to other types of good. As Walzer puts it, "in formal terms, complex equality means that no citizen's standing in one sphere or with regard to one social good can be undercut by his standing in some other sphere, with regard to some other social good".[35] From this perspective, there may be no need to limit money inequality.

Mickey Kaus agrees. In *The End of Equality*,[36] he argues for what he terms "civic liberalism", as against "money liberalism". The latter involves reducing income inequalities, the former aims to restrict the spheres of life in which money matters, and seeks to expand the public space in which money differences are ignored. He wants to boost the non-economic sphere where money cannot talk, and hold sway. Again, reducing money inequalities is not on the agenda. It is clear from the book's preface that the author, a journalist, was responding to a dilemma faced by American liberals, and in particular Bill Clinton. Like Crosland, Kaus asks how we can "pursue the traditional liberal goal of social equality at a time when, first, differences in income and wealth seem to be ineluctably growing, and, second, this money inequality increasingly originates in differences of skill and talent". The preface concludes with the observation that "Clinton presumably believes, as do many Democrats, that there is an advantage in combining money and civic liberalism. The claim of *The End of Equality*, is that this advantage is a chimera – that Clinton, or his successors, will eventually have to choose".

New Labour seems set to choose civic liberalism over money liberalism. After years of being in opposition there is not enough political will to see through an aggressive direct attack on money inequalities, by high taxation, or direct attacks on advantage such as private education. It seems clear that the focus will be on redistributing opportunities, not income – an emphasis on preventative medicine, through boosting skills, not invasive surgery, through higher taxes. Yet, if we do accept that people are capable of, and should be held responsible for, their choices we will have to concede that equal opportunities will result in unequal outcomes. Not everyone will have the natural talent to succeed, despite their efforts. Society cannot hope to fully compensate those who are disadvantaged by unequal natural abilities. But what it can ensure, which is morally most urgent, is a baseline of capability rather than a baseline of income. It matters less that public spending may benefit the middle classes, as Le Grand had argued, than the fact that it provides some measure of equality of status and some sense of a common culture. Money equality may be dead, but long live equality.

Endnotes

1. H Gaitskell (1955) "Public Ownership and Equality" in *Socialist Commentary*, June.

2. Margaret Drabble (1988) "Case for Equality", *Fabian Society* No 527.

3. C A R Crosland (1974) *Socialism Now and Other Essays*, London: Jonathan Cape.

4. D Miller (1989) "Equality" in *Philosophy and Politics* G M K Hunt.

5. *The Justice Gap*, IPPR (1993).

6. A Gutmann (1980) *Liberal Equality*, Cambridge: CUP.

7. *The Justice Gap, op cit.*

8. G Foote (1986) *The Labour Party's Political Thought*, London: Croom Helm.

9. *ibid.*

10. G B Shaw (1890) "What Socialism Is", *Fabian Society* No 13.

11. G B Shaw (1949) *The Intelligent Women's Guide to Socialism, Capitalism, Sovietism and Fascism*, London: Constable.

12. *ibid.*

13. C A R Crosland (1956) *The Future of Socialism*, London: Jonathan Cape.

14. J Raz (1986) *The Morality of Freedom*, Oxford: Clarendon Press.

15. R H Tawney (1931) *Equality*, London: Allen & Unwin.

16. *ibid.*

17. *ibid.*

18. R H Tawney (1931) *op cit.*

19. *ibid.*

20. Crosland C A R (1956) *op cit.*

21. J Rawls (1971) *A Theory of Justice*, Cambridge Mass.:Harvard University Press.

22. C A R Crosland (1974) *Socialism Now and Other Essays*, London: Jonathan Cape.

23. R Plant (1981) "Democratic Socialism and Equality" in *The Socialist Agenda: Crosland's Legacy*, edited by D Lipsey and D Leonard, London: Jonathan Cape.

24. J Rawls (1971) *op cit.*

25. N Bosanquet and P Townsend (eds) (1980) *Labour and Equality: A Fabian Study of Labour in Power 1974-1979*, London: Heinemann.

26. J Goldthorpe (1980) *Social Mobility and Class Structure in Modern Britain*, Oxford: Clarendon Press.

27. R Plant (1984) "Equality, Markets and the State", *Fabian Society* No 494.

28. *ibid.*

29. K Joseph and J Sumption (1979) *Equality*, London.

30. N Kinnock (1986) "The Future of Socialism" *Fabian Society* No 509.

31. R Hattersley (1987) *Choose Freedom: The Future for Democratic Socialism*, London: Michael Joseph.

32. J Rawls (1971) *op cit.*

33. R Hattersley (1987) *op cit.*

34. G Brown (1996) *John Smith Memorial Lecture: New Labour and Equality*, 19 April.

35. M Walzer (1983) *Spheres of Justice*, New York: Basic Books.

36. M Kaus (1992) *The End of Equality*, New York: Basic Books.

Back to Socialist Basics[1]

G A Cohen

On 24 November 1993, a meeting of Left intellectuals occurred in
London, under the auspices of the Institute for Public Policy
Research (IPPR), which is a Left-leaning think tank. A short
document was circulated in advance of the meeting, to clarify its
purpose. Among other things, the document declared that the task
of the IPPR was "to do what the Right did in the seventies, namely
to break through the prevailing parameters of debate and offer a
new perspective on contemporary British politics." The explanatory
document also said that "our concern is not to engage in a
philosophical debate about foundations of socialism."

If this meant that those foundations were not the appropriate
thing to talk about, that might have been right: not everything has
to be discussed at every meeting. But if what was meant was that
discussion of philosophical foundations is not what the Left now
needs, then I disagree, and, if that indeed is what was meant, then
I think it curious that the breakthrough by the Right should have
been invoked as an achievement for the Left to emulate. For, if there
is a lesson for the Left in the Right's breakthrough, it is that the
Left must repossess itself of its traditional foundations, on pain of
continuing along its present politically feeble reactive course. If the
Left turns its back on its foundations, it will be unable to make
statements that are truly its own.

Theory, conviction, practice

An essential ingredient in the Right's breakthrough was an
intellectual self-confidence that was grounded in fundamental
theoretical work by academics such as Milton Friedman, Friedrich
Hayek, and Robert Nozick. In one instructive sense, those authors
did not propose new ideas. Instead they explored, developed, and
forthrightly reaffirmed the Right's traditional principles. Those
principles are not so traditional to the British political Right as they

are to the American, but they are traditional nevertheless, in the important sense that they possess an historical depth which is associated with the conceptual and moral depth at which they are located.

What the Right did is not proof of what the Left should do. It is, nevertheless, extremely suggestive. It tells against looking for "a big new idea". That is a futile endeavour, since you do not land a new idea as a result of angling for one in the wide sea of intellectual possibility. New ideas standardly come from attempts to solve problems by which old ideas are stumped. Sometimes the new idea turns out to be big, but looking for a big new idea, as such, because it would be impressive to have one, is a ridiculous agendum.

The character of the Right's success suggests that if, as the IPPR document also said, and as I agree, customary inherited socialist rhetoric now turns people off, then the remedy is not to cast about for a different rhetoric, or buzz-phrase, irrespective of what its relationship to traditional principles may be, but to restore our own contact with those principles, from which exercise a new rhetoric may indeed emerge. The old rhetoric now sounds dated not because everybody knows the content behind it but partly because its content has been forgotten. The Left will not recoup itself ideologically without addressing that foundational content.

The relationship between theory and practice is more complex than some friends of the Labour party appear now to suppose. The point of theory is not to generate a comprehensive social design which the politician then seeks to implement. Things do not work that way, because implementing a design requires whole cloth, and nothing in contemporary politics is made out of whole cloth. Politics is an endless struggle, and theory serves as a weapon in that struggle, because it provides a characterisation of its direction, and of its controlling purpose.

Considered as practical proposals, the theories of Friedman, Hayek and Nozick were crazy; crazy in the strict sense that you would have to be crazy to think that such proposals (eg abolition of *all* regulation of professional standards and of safety at work, abolition of state money, abolition of *all* welfare provision) might be implemented in the short, medium, or long term.[2] The theories are in that sense crazy precisely because they are uncompromisingly fundamental: they were not devised with one eye on electoral possibility. And just for that reason, their serviceability in electoral and other political contest is very great. *Politicians and activists can press not-so-crazy right-wing proposals with conviction because they have the strength of conviction that depends upon depth of conviction, and depth comes from theory that is too fundamental to be practicable in a direct sense.*

I said that politicians make nothing out of whole cloth. All change in modern conditions of social differentiation and international integration is perforce incremental, one per cent here, five per cent there, accumulating after, say, fifteen years, into a revolution. The large fundamental values help to power (or block) the little changes by nourishing the justificatory rhetoric which is needed to push (or resist) change. Fundamental socialist values which point to a form of society a hundred miles from the horizon of present possibility are needed to defend every half-mile of territory gained and to mount an attempt to regain each bit that has been lost.

Consider Gordon Brown's response to Kenneth Clarke's budget of November 1993. Its central themes were two: the Tories have broken their promise not to raise taxes, and it is they who are responsible for the mess which obliged them to break that promise. That combined charge, important though it is, and important as it was to level it, requires no socialist value, no non-Tory value, to back it up. Consider, too, Michael Portillo's artful manoeuvre around Brown's charge. He did not have to face it in its own terms because he could say with conviction to Brown that Brown proposed no solution to the £50 billion deficit (to which Brown's criticisms of betrayal and incompetence and Brown's policy of long-term greater investment indeed represented no solution). Brown centred his attack on the misdemeanours of economic mismanagement and political promise-breaking, instead of on the crime of depressing the conditions of life of poor people, and on the crime of not loading more burden on the better off, including the not stupendously well off. I do not say that Brown did not mention the sheer inegalitarianism of the budget's profile. But he did not and could not make that point with conviction as a central point, because he is imprisoned by the thought about who votes for what and because he has lost touch with foundational values.

The Brown response was relatively ineffectual partly because it presupposed for its effect that people are dumber than they actually are. People already knew that the Tories made the mess, though it was no doubt useful to remind them of it, to keep it at the forefront of their consciousness. But they are not so dumb that they think it follows from the fact that the Tories made the mess that Labour would be better at getting the country out of it. Labour will win the politics of competence only if people have confidence in its competence. That requires that Labour itself be confident in its own superior competence, and that in turn requires that it be confident in itself, *tout court*, which it can only be if it transcends its furtive relationship to its traditional values. Electoral success is to a large extent a by-product of commitment to something other than electoral success.

Success in a particular election can, moreover, be bought at the cost of an ideological backslide which has lasting deleterious effect. It is one thing to point out that the Tories have failed by their own standards. It is quite another, in the course of making that good point, to endorse those standards yourself. Labour is now so beguiled by the prospect of exposing the Tories as tax-raisers that it is beginning to treat tax restraint not merely as a Tory goal but as an intrinsic desideratum. Therewith traditional pledges to reinforce and extend welfare provision are being seriously compromised.[3]

Principle and politics

In its ideologically self-confident phase, when its relationship to its values was forthright rather than furtive, the Labour party affirmed a principle of community and a principle of equality. ("Community" and "equality" can be defined in different ways, and I shall say what I mean by them, as names of traditional mainstream Labour values, in the following sections). Each principle was regarded as authoritative in its own right, but also as justified through its connection with the other. Each value supported the other, and each was strengthened by the fact that it was supported by the other. And these values were not only central to the Labour party and to the wider Labour movement surrounding it. They were also the values that distinguished Labour from other parties at Westminster. They were, indeed, the only values which *the Left affirmed as a matter of principle and which the Centre and Right reject as a matter of principle.*[4]

The values of community and equality were articulated in books and pamphlets. But they were also carried by, and they expressed the sentiments of, a broad movement that no longer exists and that will never be recreated. It will never be recreated because technological change means that the class base of that movement is gone, forever. Socialist values have lost their mooring in capitalist social structure. Partly because of that, but also partly because of right-wing ideological successes, community and equality have lost the quite extensive ideological hegemony that they once enjoyed. If I had to hazard a causal story, I would say that right-wing values filled a space vacated by left-wing values which went on vacation because their class base was eroded. Because I think that is a likely causal story, I should not be accused of accusing Labour's leaders of gratuitous betrayal, in their abandonment of traditional values. "Betrayal" is the wrong name for abandonment which has a hard underlying social cause. But the hardness of the cause does not mean that there is no alternative but to allow wholesale abandonment of values to be its effect.

The struggle for community and equality is perforce more difficult when the calculus of class interest reduces the constituency that would gain from them, in an immediate sense of "gain". But there remain two reasons for insisting on their authority. The first, which is decisive on its own, is a self-standing moral-cum-intellectual reason. The second, more contingent and debatable, is a reason related to the identity and survival of the Labour party, and it is contingent partly because it is not a necessary truth that the Labour party should continue to exist.

The decisive reason for not abandoning community and equality is that the moral force of those values never depended on the social force supporting them that is now disappearing. No one who believed in the values could have said that she believed in them *because* they expressed the sentiments of a social movement. Anyone who believed in them believed in them because she thought them inherently authoritative, and the withering of the social force that backed them cannot justify ceasing to think them authoritative. And the second reason for not abandoning the values is that, once they are dropped, then there is no reason of principle, as opposed to of history, for Labour not to merge with the Liberal Democrats. Labour cannot cherish its independence as a party, believe in a politics of principle, and affirm nothing but the "four principles of social justice" affirmed in *The Justice Gap* and *Social Justice in a Changing World*.[5] No Liberal Democrat or progressive Tory need reject those principles.[6]

A different response to the present predicament is to think the values afresh in a spirit of loyalty to them and in order to see how one can sustain commitment to them in an inhospitable time, and what new modes of advocacy of them are possible. But that partly practical task requires foundational reflection of just the sort that the IPPR might have meant us to eschew.[7]

You can ask what our principles are, what, that is, we believe with passion, and you can ask what is the best way to win the next election. But you cannot ask what principles we should have, and what we should believe with passion, as a means of winning the next election.[8] For the answer will not be principles you can really believe in, and you might therefore not even help yourself electorally, since electors are not so unperceptive that they can be relied upon not to notice that you are dissembling.

The two IPPR documents bow before the success of pro-market and anti-egalitarian ideology that has helped to precipitate Labour's present ideological crisis. There is, as I have said, nothing in their four "core ideas"[9] that any Liberal Democrat or left-wing Tory need reject. To be sure, the Tories in particular do not in practice respect the core ideas as much as a Labour government might, but that does not justify flourishing forth pale principles to define the direction of Labour's renewal.

After each of Labour's four electoral failures, the Labour Right said: we did not win because we looked too socialist; and the Labour Left said: we did not win because we did not look socialist enough. I do not think either side knows that what it claims to be true is true, and, if one side is right, then I do not know which is.[10] Certainly there exists an aversion to increases in taxation, and although that is no doubt partly because no truly principled defence of greater redistribution is confidently projected, I admit that I do not know how large a part of the explanation of unpopularity of greater taxation is associated with failure to project is justification. I am therefore not contending that a principled defence of community and equality is a sure route to electoral success in 1997. But failure to secure acceptance of the principles of community and equality[11] is not a reason to modify one's *belief* in the principles themselves, even if it is indeed a reason, politics being what it is, not to thrust them forward publicly in their unvarnished form.[12] To massage one's beliefs for the sake of electoral gain can, moreover, be electorally counterproductive. It can be inexpedient to abandon principle for expediency, because it is hard to hide the fact that you are doing so, and everyone, Neil Kinnock included, knew that the Tories were right when, to powerful electoral effect, they accused Kinnock of that unprincipled abandonment. The Commission on Social Justice should not pretend to run an exercise in the examination of principle whose real focus is not principle but electoral success, because then it will certainly betray principle and possibly contribute to electoral failure.

Community versus market

I mean here, by "community", the anti-market principle according to which I serve you not because of what I can get out of doing so but because you need my service.[13] That is anti-market because the market motivates productive contribution not on the basis of commitment to one's fellow human beings and a desire to service them while being served *by* them, but on the basis of impersonal cash reward. The immediate motive to productive activity in a market society is typically[14] some mixture of greed and fear, in proportions that vary with the details of a person's market position and personal character. In greed, other people are seen as possible sources of enrichment, and in fear they are seen as threats. These are horrible ways of seeing other people, however much we have been habituated and inured to them, as a result of centuries of capitalist development.[15]

I said that, in community motivation, I produce because of my commitment to my fellow human beings and with a desire to serve them while being served by them.[16] In such motivation, there is indeed an expectation of reciprocation, but it nevertheless differs critically from market motivation. The marketeer is willing to serve, but only in order to be served. He does not desire the conjunction (serve-and-be-served) as such, for he would not serve if doing so were not a means to get service. The difference is expressed in the lack of the fine tuning that attends non-market motivation. Contrast taking turns in a loose way with respect to who buys the drinks with keeping a record of who has paid what for them. The former procedure is in line with community, the latter with the market.

Now, the history of the twentieth century encourages the thought that the easiest way to generate productivity in a modern society is by nourishing the motives of greed and fear, in a hierarchy of unequal income. That does not make them attractive motives. Who would propose running a society on such motives, and thereby promoting the psychology to which they belong, if they were not known to be effective, did they not have the instrumental value which is the only value that they have? In the famous statement in which Adam Smith justified market relations, he pointed out that we place our faith not in the butcher's generosity, but on his self interest, when we rely on him to provision us. Smith thereby propounded a wholly extrinsic justification of market motivation, in face of what he acknowledged to be its unattractive intrinsic character. Traditional socialists have often ignored Smith's point, in a moralistic condemnation of market motivation which fails to address its extrinsic justification. Certain contemporary over-enthusiastic market socialists tend, contrariwise, to forget that the market is intrinsically repugnant, because they are blinded by their belated discovery of the market's extrinsic value. The genius of the market is that it recruits shabby motives to desirable ends, and, in a balanced view, both sides of that proposition must be kept in focus.

Generosity *and* self-interest exist in everyone. We know how to make an economic system work on the basis of self-interest. We do not know how to make it work on the basis of generosity. But that does not mean that we should forget generosity: we should still confine the sway of self-interest as much as we can. We do that, for example, when we tax, redistributively, the unequalising results of market activity. The extent to which we can do that without defeating our aim (of making the badly off better off) varies inversely with the extent to which self-interest has been allowed to triumph in private and public consciousness.[17] (To the extent that self-interest has indeed triumphed, heavily progressive taxation drives high earners abroad, or causes them to decide to reduce their labour input, or induces in them a morose attitude which makes their previous input hard or impossible to sustain.)

The market, any market, contradicts the principle which not only Marx but his socialist predecessors proclaimed for the good society, the principle embodied in the slogan "from each according to his ability, to each according to his needs." One might ask what it means for each to give according to his ability, and what it means for each to get according to his needs. But for present purposes, the unambiguous message of the slogan is that what you get is *not* a function of what you give, that contribution and benefit are separate matters. Here the relationship between people is not the instrumental one in which I give because I get, but the wholly non-instrumental one in which I give because you need. You do not get more because you produce more, and you do not get less because you are not good at producing. Accordingly, the ideal in the primeval socialist slogan constitutes a complete rejection of the logic of the market.

The socialist aspiration was to extend community to the whole of our economic life. We now know that we do not now know how to do that, and many think that we now know that it is impossible to do that. But community conquests in certain domains, such as health care and education, have sustained viable forms of production and distribution in the past, and it is consequently a matter for regret that the IPPR documents do not invoke community as a core value, when it is a value that is currently under aggressive threat from the market principle, and when then there is even immediate political mileage to be got from reasserting community in the mentioned particular domains.

Justice and equality

The principle of equality says that the amount of amenity and burden in one person's life should be roughly comparable to that in any other's. That principle is not mentioned in the documents;

or, to be more precise, it is mentioned only in parody, in the statement that "few people believe in arithmetical equality".[18] Perhaps no one believes in the unlimited sway of the principle of equality, as I defined it above,[19] where, that is, equality is rough similarity of amenity and burden. But I, and many others, certainly believe in it as a value to be traded off against others, and this value is rejected, as such, in the Commission's documents. Instead, we have an arrestingly weak proposition – strangely said to be a "radical" one[20] – in the fourth "core idea" of social justice, which reads as follows: "Inequalities are not necessarily unjust – but those which are should be reduced and where possible eliminated."[21] Those who are eager to declare their support for unjust inequalities will oppose the fourth core idea.

Proposition three on social justice reads, in part, as follows:

> Redistribution of income is a means to social justice and not an end in itself; social justice demands sufficient revenue to meet basic needs and extend opportunities, but there are limits of principle as well as practice to levels of taxation.[22]

To say that (an equalising) redistribution of income is not an end in itself but only a means to fulfil basic needs and extend opportunities, is once again, to abandon equality as a principle.[23]

The fourth core idea and the third proposition on social justice raise two questions: first, what is the difference between a just and an unjust inequality? And, second, what are the "limits of principle" to taxation, beyond which taxation counts as "punitive?"[24]

An answer to the first question is given on page 43 of *The Justice Gap*. The inequalities that "are indeed justified"[25] are, it says there, justified by "need, merit, or reward"[26] I find that list curious and I want to examine it in a little detail.

"Inequalities" justified in terms of need are not ones that even the most radical egalitarian has ever opposed. *The Justice Gap* does not say what needs it contemplates here, but there are only two kinds that appear relevant. First, some people need more resources to achieve the same level of well-being as others. But to unequalise resources on that basis is consistent with egalitarianism of a most radical kind. Second, some people need more means of production than others do to carry out their social function. But producer need is out of place in a roll-call of justified inequalities which is intended to challenge an uncompromising egalitarianism. No egalitarian thinks that brain surgeons should be denied expensive equipment.

The other supposed ways of justifying inequalities are, first, in terms of merit and, second, in terms of reward. But the phrase "inequality justified in terms of reward" conveys no clear thought, especially when it is, as here, contrasted with "inequality justified in terms of merit." I suppose that the phrase was a piece of innocent carelessness, yet it is symptomatic of the altogether casual treatment of equality in these proceedings that such carelessness should have got by the eyes of what must have been quite a few readers. I presume we can take it that what was intended by "inequality justified in terms of reward" is inequality justified in terms of reward for merit and/or effort. So let me address merit and effort, as grounds of inequality.

If one person produces more than others that is because he is more talented or because he expends more effort or because he is lucky in his circumstances of production, which is to say that he is lucky with respect to whom and what he produces *with*. The last reason for greater productivity, lucky circumstance is morally (as opposed to economically) unintelligible as a reason for greater reward. And whereas rewarding productivity which is due to greater inherent talent is indeed morally intelligible, from certain ethical standpoints, it is nevertheless a profoundly anti-socialist idea, correctly stigmatised by J S Mill as an instance of "giving to those who have",[27] since greater talent is itself a piece of fortune that calls for no further reward.

Effort might be a different matter. I say that it *might* be different, because it can be contended that unusual effort (largely) reflects unusual capacity for effort, which is but a further form of talent and therefore subject to the same scepticism as talent itself is with respect to its relevance to reward. But let us allow, against such scepticism, that effort is indeed *pertinently*[28] subject to the will. That being granted, ask, now, why the effortful person who is supposed to be handsomely rewarded expended the effort she did. Did she do so in order to enrich herself? If so, then why should her special effort command a high reward? Or did she work hard in order to benefit others? If so, then it contradicts her own aim to reward her with extra resources that others would otherwise have, as opposed to with a salute and a handshake and a sense of gratitude.[29] Those remarks are, of course, only the beginning of a long argument, but it is indicative of the utter conventionality of the disparagement of equality in the IPPR pamphlets that such considerations lie beyond their horizon.[30]

I turn to the question raised by the third proposition on social justice,[31] concerning the "limits of principle on taxation". Now, although those "limits of principle" are not defined or explained in the two published documents, I conjecture that part[32] of the unstated explanation of them is the one that appears in the unpublished paper on "Ideas of Social Justice" that Bernard Williams prepared for the Commission. Echoing a chief claim of Robert Nozick's, Williams said that "sustaining as equal distribution of money would involve continuous incursions into liberty."

That summary remark overlooks the conceptual truth that to have money is (pro tanto) to have liberty. The richer you are, the more courses of action are open to you, which is to say that you are freer than you would be otherwise. Accordingly, whoever receives money as a result of redistribution thereby enjoys an enhancement of her liberty,[33] albeit at the expense of the liberty of the person from whom it is taken, but with the net result for liberty as such entirely moot. Taxation restricts not, as it is here misleadingly suggested, liberty as such, but private property rights, both in external things and in one's own labour power. Whether or not such rights are deeply founded, it is ideological hocus-pocus to identify them with liberty as such, and it is entirely alien to traditional socialist belief so to construe them.

The stout opposition to equality and redistribution as matters of principle is revealed in this rejection of Tory dogma:

Contrary to the "trickle-down" theory of the 1980s, making the rich richer does not make the poor richer too. Indeed, because the great majority pay the costs of unemployment, crime and ill-health, making the poor poorer makes us all poorer too. Common interests demand social cohesion rather than polarisation.[34]

This appeal side-steps the politically difficult redistributive issue. By plausible absolute standards, most people in the past were poor, and the target for redistribution could then be a rich minority. Now, by the same absolute standards, the standards in the light of which it is pertinently pointed out that 62 per cent of UK households have videos,[35] only a minority are poor. To appeal to the self interest of the majority (dressed up as an interest they have in common with the poor) as a central reason for relieving the poverty of that minority may work electorally: that depends on how the electoral majority do the arithmetic the appeal invites them to engage in. It depends, that is, on whether they will reckon that higher taxation is a smaller price to pay for their own health and security than what they would have to shell out on BUPA, improved anti-burglary systems, a house in the suburbs, and so on. But however they figure those sums, inviting them to consider the issue primarily in that framework,[36] under a pretence of common interest, is a cop-out at the level of principle.

Appendix: on money and liberty

A standard political debate runs as follows. The Right extols the freedom enjoyed by all in a liberal capitalist society. The Left complains that the freedom in question is meagre for poor people. The Right rejoins that the Left confuses freedom with resources. You are free to do what no one will interfere with your doing, says the Right. If you cannot afford to do it that does not mean that someone will interfere with your doing it, but just that you lack the means or ability to do it. The problem the poor face is lack of ability, not lack of freedom. The Left may then say that ability should count for as much as freedom does. The Right can then reply, to significant political effect: so *you* may think, but our priority is freedom.

In my view, the depicted right-wing stance depends upon a reified view of money. Money is unlike intelligence or physical strength, poor endowments of which do not, indeed, prejudice freedom, where freedom is understood as absence of interference. The difference between money and those endowments implies, I shall argue, that lack of money *is* (a form of) lack of freedom, in the favoured sense of freedom, where it is taken to be absence of interference.[37]

To see this, begin by imagining a society without money, in which courses of action available to people, courses they are free to follow without interference, are laid down by the law. The law says what each sort of person, or even each particular person, may and may not do without interference, and each person is endowed with a set of tickets detailing what she is allowed to do. So I may have a ticket saying that I am free to plough this land, another one saying that I am free to go to that opera, or to walk across that field, while you have different tickets, with different freedoms inscribed on them.

Imagine, now, that the structure of the options written on the tickets is more complex. Each ticket lays out a disjunction of conjunctions of courses of action that I may perform. I may do A and B and C and D *or* B and C and D and E *or* E and F and G and A, and so on. If I try to do something not licensed by my ticket or tickets, armed force intervenes.

By hypothesis, these tickets say what my freedoms (and, consequently, my unfreedoms) are. But a sum of money is nothing but a highly generalised form of such a ticket. A sum of money is a licence to perform a disjunction of conjunctions of actions – actions, like, for example, visiting one's sister in Bristol, or taking home, and wearing, the sweater on the counter at Selfridges.

Suppose that someone is too poor to visit her sister in Bristol. She cannot save, from week to week, enough to buy her way there. Then, as far as her freedom is concerned, that is equivalent to "trip to Bristol" not being written on someone's ticket in the imagined non-monetary economy. The woman I've described has the capacity to go to Bristol. She can board the underground and approach the barrier she must cross to reach the train. But she will be physically prevented from passing through it, or physically ejected from the train, or, in the other example, she will be physically stopped outside Selfridges and the sweater will be removed. The only way you won't be prevented from getting and using things is by offering money for them.

To have money *is* to have freedom, and the assimilation of money to mental and bodily resources is a piece of unthinking fetishism, in the good old Marxist sense that it misrepresents *social relations of constraint as things* that people lack. In a word: money is no object.[38]

Endnotes

1. First appeared in New Left Review 207, (Sept/Oct 1994), p6.

2. Profoundly transforming though the Thatcher revolution has been, the distance between British society now and the standards set by right-wing theory remains enormous.

3   Cf. the excellent article by David McKie on p. 18 of *The Guardian* for 31 January 1994, one paragraph of which runs as follows: "Unless it is handled with extreme deftness, Labour's present campaign is in danger of shoring up the classic Thatcherite picture of taxation as something inherently undesirable, even wicked; something that shackles opportunity rather than, as Labour once taught, expanding it by building the public services on which the great majority of voters and their families will always need to depend: safeguarding *your* health, *your* welfare, *your* children's education."

4. "X rejects V as a matter of principle" means, here, "X rejects V when it is put as a matter of principle", and *not* "It is a matter of principle, for X, to reject V."

    You could disagree with the italicised claim in either of two ways. You might think that one or both of the values I've identified don't fit the italicised description, or you might think that some value which I've not identified does. I'll be more surprised if you're able to disagree in the second way, not, that is, by challenging the distinguishing role of the values I've identified, but by claiming that a value not identified here also enjoyed such a role. (Perhaps a third such value, as suggested to me by Danny Goldstick, is equality of power, in a political sense, as opposed to equality in the economic-distributive sense which occupies me here. This value was indeed affirmed by the Left. But I doubt that it was rejected by both the Right and the Centre.)

5. Both *The Justice Gap* and *Social Justice in a Changing World* emanated from the Commission on Social Justice and were published by the IPPR in 1993. The present essay was prompted by the consternation and, sometimes, shock that I experienced when reading the two documents.

6. The four "principles" (*The Justice Gap*, pp. i, 16) or "key ideas" (*Social Justice in a Changing World* p. i) or "core ideas" (*Social Justice in a Changing World*, p. 4): "1. The foundation of a free society is the equal worth of all citizens. 2. All citizens should be able as a right of citizenship to meet their basic needs for income, shelter, education, nutrition and health care. 3. Self-respect and personal autonomy depend on the widest possible spread of opportunities and life-chances. 4. Inequalities are not necessarily unjust but unjustified inequalities should be reduced and where possible eliminated" (*Social Justice in a Changing World*, p. 4). In a somewhat different formulation of principle 4, given at *The Justice Gap* p. i, it reads: "4. Inequalities are not necessarily unjust – but those which are should be reduced and where possible eliminated.'

7. See page 29 above.

8. My own claim that reaffirmation of traditional values would have electoral force is not put as an answer to that counterfeit question. My view that the old principles can be electorally supportive does not imply the (incoherent) recommendation that we should believe in them *because* they can be supportive, even though it does imply rejection of an electorally inspired case for abandoning them.

9. *Social Justice in a Changing World* p 4.

10. Has there been a post-electoral survey of potential Labour voters who did not vote Labour to determine how many voted otherwise, or abstained, for each of the stated opposite reasons? (Not that what people say in such a survey is conclusive with respect to what their response to a different campaign would have been.)

11. And, some might add, especially a failure which followed hardly any attempt to defend them.

12. Politics (again) being what it is, a gap between belief and public statement is often unavoidable. But there is a limit to how big that gap can be, without compromising both principle and political effectiveness, and when the gap approaches that limit, principle forbids adjusting belief, as opposed to public statement.

13. That is by no means the only thing that "community" can mean. Nor do I regard it as a particularly good name for what I use it to name here: I simply haven't been able to think of a better one.

14. People can operate under a sense of service even in a market society, but, insofar as they do, what makes the market work is not what makes them work. Their discipline is not market

discipline. (Some think that the very success of the market depends on the tempering leaven within it of non-capitalist motivation: for present purposes, there is no need to form a judgement about that complex claim.)

15. Capitalism did not, of course, invent greed and fear: they are deep in human nature, related as they are to elementary infantile structures. But capitalism has undoubtedly magnified the role of greed in particular in ordinary life, and, unlike its predecessor feudal civilisation, which had the (Christian) grace to condemn greed, capitalism celebrates it.

16. Under its most abstract description, the motivation in question might be consistent with hierarchy: Prince Charles's motto is *Ich dien*, and serfs and lords alike who buy feudal ideology wholesale can describe themselves as being motivated thus. If community motivation is indeed consistent with hierarchy, then the principle of equality informs the principle of community, in its socialist form.

17. My views on this matter run alongside those of John Stuart Mill, who averred that "[e]verybody has selfish and unselfish interests, and a selfish man has cultivated the habit of caring for the former, and not caring for the latter." And one thing that contributes to the direction in which a person's habits develop is the ambient social ethos, which is influenced by the stance of political leaders. (The Mill quotation is from his *Considerations on Representative Government,* in J. M. Robson, ed., *The Collected Works of John Stuart Mill,* Toronto 1965-86, Volume 19, p. 444. For sapient commentary on this and other relevant passages in Mill, see Richard Ashcraft, "Class Conflict and Constitutionalism in J S Mill's thought", in Nancy Rosenblum (ed.) (1989), *Liberalism and the Moral Life,* Cambridge, Mass., pp. 117-18.)

18. *The Justice Gap* p. ii. *op cit.*

19. For a more precise definition of the principle, see my "On the Currency of Egalitarian Justice", *Ethics,* vol. 99, 1989.

20. *The Justice Gap* p i *op cit.*

21. *ibid.*

22. *Social Justice in a Changing World,* p. 24 (cf. *The Justice Gap,* p. 13). This is not one of the "four principles of social justice" listed in reference 5 above, but one of the "ten propositions on social justice" which are more specific and more circumstantial than the four principles are.

23. Notice that to say that equalising redistribution of income is an end in itself is not to say that the equality to be achieved thereby is of income, as opposed to, for example, of what Amartya Sen calls "capability".

24. *Social Justice in a Changing World*, p. 25 *op cit.*

25. And, therefore, in conformity with justice, since – see the end of reference 5 above – "just" and "justified", which can convey different ideas, are used interchangeably in the IPPR documents.

26. cf., *The Justice Gap* p.15 *op cit.*

27. *Principles of Political Economy*, in J M Robson, ed., *op cit.*, Volume 2. p. 210.

28. I emphasise "pertinently", because, among those who agree that effort is subject to the will, some ("hard determinists") would deny that raises a challenge to egalitarian views of distributive justice, and others (eg Rawls) issue the same denial, on the non-determinist basis that it is inscrutable to what extent a person's emission of effort is not due to differential good fortune. (For a critical discussion of Rawls's remarks on effort, see section III of my "On the Currency of Egalitarian Justice", *op. cit.*)

29. Or, indeed, with a sum of money, conceived as a gift expressing gratitude, rather than as an ex ante motivating reward.

30. The two most influential Anglophone political philosophy books of recent years are John Rawls's *Theory of Justice*, (1971), Cambridge, Mass., which is left liberal, and Robert Nozick's *Anarchy, State and Utopia*, (1974), New York, which is extreme free-market Right. It conforms to the outlook of these documents that Rawls should be cited critically and Nozick positively, with respect to their teachings about equality. Nozick's discovery that one does not have to deserve one's talent to deserve the fruits of its exercise is heartily commended (*The Justice Gap*, p.13), while the egalitarian Rawlsian reminder that talent is but good fortune is disparaged, and, moreover, misrepresented as a premise for the plainly false conclusion, which Rawls does not assert, that "in the last analysis all that anyone's work represents is a site at which society has achieved something" (*The Justice Gap* p. 13). The single moderately extended exposition of academic political philosophy in these documents serves to make an anti-egalitarian point in a slapdash way.

31. See page 4 above.

32. Another part, presumably, is the idea that too much taxation trenches against the claims of "need, merit or reward': see p4 above.

33. For further demonstration of the connection between money and liberty see the Appendix to this chapter.

34. *Social Justice in a Changing World*, p. 22. The statement is part of the elaboration of the first "proposition on social justice", which reads as follows: "Social justice is about more than poverty – it concerns everyone. The best way to help the minority who are poor is to advance social justice for all."

35. *The Justice Gap*, p. 19 *op cit.*

36. As the amalgam consisting of the first proposition on social justice (see reference 33 above), and its complete elaboration does.

37. Accordingly, poverty should not be bracketed with illness and lack of education and thereby be treated as a restriction on "what [people] can do with their freedom" (*The Justice Gap*, p. 8). Poverty restricts freedom itself, and the Left needlessly accedes the Right's misrepresentation of the relationship between poverty and freedom when it issues statements like that just quoted. Cf. John Rawls *A Theory of Justice*, p. 204: "The inability to take advantage of one's rights and opportunities as a result of poverty and ignorance, and a lack of means generally, is sometimes counted among the constraints definitive of liberty. I shall not however, say this, but rather I shall think of these things as affecting the worth of liberty ..."

38. I thank Arnold Zubboff for extended, patient criticism of an earlier draft of this paper. I am also grateful for written comments from Alan Carling, Paula Casal, Norman Geras, Keith Graham, John McMurtry, David Miller, John Roemer, Amélie Rorty, Hillel Steiner, Bernard Williams and Erik Wright.

Forward to Basics
Bernard Williams

Introduction

In his paper *Back to Socialist Basics*, Jerry Cohen has mounted a spirited assault on the approach which was adopted by the Commission on Social Justice and was expressed in its Report and in its two earlier publications *The Justice Gap* and *Social Justice in a Changing World*. The present essay, though it will probably do nothing to alleviate his "consternation and shock", is a personal attempt to explain why people on the Left have no need to share these reactions; and why, if they do share them, they should direct them at the world, not at the Commission.

There are three things, at least, in Cohen's paper with which I agree. The first is that those, such as the Commission, who are trying to think about policies for the Left should address themselves to principles, not just to electoral success. One reason for this is that electoral success itself requires one to be convincing, and being convincing is not unconnected with having convictions. However, while political success should not and cannot be uniquely the objective, its prospects should not be despised as an indicator. If the electorate cannot be persuaded to support one, one needs to ask why this is. There are some answers to this question which need not lead one to question one's principles, and the Left has, for obvious reasons, been keen to find such answers. Some of those answers have no doubt, on various occasions, been correct. But sometimes the disappointed Left offers not much more than a moralising disappointment with the electors, to the effect that they are too greedy and self-centred to accept one's principles, and then the time has come to ask whether one's principles are principles for these people – whether, indeed, they are *political* principles at all.

Second, I agree with Cohen that principles involve, in a certain sense, foundations. I indeed agree that they involve traditional foundations,[1] inasmuch as no-one could reasonably hope to persuade people of a political outlook which had no roots in historical experience. It remains to be seen, however, in any given case what is the tradition in question and how it is to be interpreted. In particular, the tradition relevant to a political movement need not necessarily be its "manifest tradition" – that is, roughly, what people think of first if they think schematically about its past. If the phrase "traditional values" works merely as a trigger of nostalgia, it will be no less a deceptive device in the Labour party than it usually has been in the Tory party.

Third, I agree broadly with Cohen about the relation of ideas or political values to policy: principles do not generate blue-prints, but rather convey a unifying sense that gives life to policies. I also agree that pictures of social life that convey values may well be influential without being practicable – they may be in a way crazy. Cohen cites certain images that have been influentially offered by the Right in the past twenty years. However, I do not agree with his account – which, so far as I can see, he simply takes for granted – of why they were influential. He assumes that it is because they were traditional. But they were not traditional – quite certainly not in Britain, where *laissez-faire* capitalism has not been for the most part the central motivating idea of the Conservative party. We have to look elsewhere for the power of these ideas, and there are several directions in which we can look. One of the less encouraging explanations of why these ideas have had an effect is that they are in a certain sense psychologically and historically realistic; although the schemes of theorists such as Nozick or Hayek are themselves unrealistic, they may be seen as appealing to motives that people have and are not ashamed to have, rather than to motives that moralists would prefer them to have. I am not endorsing that explanation. I am merely saying that there needs to be an explanation, and that the assumption from which Cohen starts, that the principles of the new Right were influential because they were at the heart of the Right's manifest tradition, is false. It is therefore no basis for the anyway pretty feeble inference that the Left will be influential only if it appeals to its manifest tradition.

Equality, desert, justice, and luck

Cohen refers to what he calls "the disparagement of equality"[2] in the Commission's publications, but it is absurd to say that the Commission "disparaged" equality. The Commission did raise some questions about what equality is, and what it should be equality of. Anyone who has equality as a political aim is faced with these questions, and no-one can take the content of that aim to be obvious.

Cohen criticises the Commission's reference to inequalities being justified by "need, merit or reward"[3] – where the last means, of course, that the justification lies in someone's being rewarded for something that he or she has achieved or contributed, where this is not necessarily a recognition of merit. If the reason for someone's greater productivity (to use Cohen's term) lies in lucky circumstances rather than in greater talent or effort, this luck, Cohen says, "is morally ... unintelligible as a reason for greater reward". But no-one proposes that the luck is the reason for the reward. The reason for the reward is the contribution, achievement, or (in Cohen's terms) production. The circumstances that enabled this to come about were indeed a matter of luck. But so, the Commission suggested, may be talents or the capacity to make an effort. Cohen seems not to disagree with this (though he may make some exceptions for efforts of will).

What he does disagree with is the way in which one should think about this. The Commission cited Nozick's question: does desert have to go "all the way down" – that is to say, can we deserve rewards for what our talents have enabled us to do, even though we do not deserve our talents? Cohen finds this shocking, not because the question is irrelevant, but because it was Nozick who asked it. But if he thinks that (roughly speaking) desert rests on what are ultimately matters of luck, and he also thinks, contrary to Nozick, that "desert must go all the way down", he must think (roughly) that nobody deserves anything. This is what Rawls thinks. I fail to see why this is misrepresented, as Cohen claims,[4] by the Commission's formulation, "... all that anyone's work represents is a site at which society has achieved something". More importantly, I fail to see why it should be regarded as morally unintelligible to deny this, and to accept that people can deserve or be entitled to rewards in virtue of what they have done, even if what they do depends on talents which they are lucky to possess.

Another contributor to this volume, Stuart White, agrees with those – I take it they include Cohen – who hold that an inequality in (say) income is unjust if it is attributable to differential "brute luck" – that is to factors that impact differentially on the prospects of individuals, but which are essentially beyond the control and influence of the individuals in question.[5] (This makes very clear, incidentally, the extent to which, if one insists on formulating the ideal of equality in such terms, one dangerously exposes it to scepticism, of much the same kind as threatens ambitious conceptions of freewill. Why is it not a matter of brute luck what people can control and influence – what, indeed, they can get themselves to control and influence? It cannot be a good idea that basic political ideas, which have to stand up to very rough treatment, should be so metaphysically sensitive.)

White accepts that a person's talents may well be, to a considerable extent, a matter of brute luck, and I take it that he must agree with Cohen (and disagree with Nozick) in thinking that desert "goes all the way down", since he concludes, against the Commission, that desert does not provide a very persuasive basis on which to reject the brute luck principle.[6] White does not himself support a "comprehensive" version of the principle, but settles for a "threshold" version. The threshold version of the brute luck principle in itself seems not to demand very much: "that we prevent, or correct/compensate for, brute luck disadvantage in strategic goods insofar as this pushes people below certain decency thresholds in their prospects for well-being and agency." You do not need to be much of an egalitarian to agree that no-one should fall below the level of decency – you merely need to be moderately human. The connection with egalitarianism, to the extent that there is one, is made, rather, by White's insistence that the threshold should be set fairly high.

This leaves an issue of principle. The original statement of the "brute luck" principle said we must consciously regulate the distribution of strategic goods such as income and wealth so as to correct and compensate for brute luck inequalities. To the extent that the threshold will fall short of the comprehensive ideal, does White think that to this extent its results will be unjust? Is this an example of a conflict of political values, one in which other political values, such as autonomy, exact a price which has to be paid by social justice?

I would rather say that when we reject some of the demands that would be made by comprehensive egalitarianism, there is perhaps less equality than there would have been, but this does not necessarily mean less justice, since there are principles of social justice other than equality. Many people would say that these include some ideas of desert, such as the idea that people can be entitled to rewards which are based on things achieved by their talents. This itself is – or would be, if properly spelled out – a principle of justice. If we accept this, and also accept the plain truth that we do not deserve our talents, then we must agree with Nozick that desert does not "go all the way down": we can deserve rewards for what our talents have enabled us to do, even though we do not deserve our talents.

In relation to the ideal of equality, we can then say either one of two different things. We may say that the ideal of equality is opposed to acknowledging the effects of brute luck at any level; in that case, equality will have no time for desert, and to the extent that we recognise desert, to that extent we reject or limit the ideal of equality. Alternatively, we may say that the ideal of equality itself should not be dedicated to cancelling the effects of brute luck at *every* level: it must confine itself to some kinds of bad luck, such as the familiar kinds of bad luck that just happen to one, and such things as the effects of disability with regard to basic capabilities. On that understanding, the recognition of certain kinds of desert could itself be consistent with the principles of equality.

There is much to be said about each of these options. The main point here, however, is that whichever way we go, we shall have to agree to two things: that equality as a political ideal needs interpreting; and that in interpreting it, we have to attend to other political values, some of which may be other principles of justice. We cannot simply assume that a recognition of desert betrays the aims of social justice.

Community and the manifest tradition

Cohen identifies the tradition of the Labour party in terms of community and equality; and it is clear, I think, that he not only regards community as a core value,[7] but also interprets equality in terms of it.

As a criticism of the Commission's principles, Cohen says that "no Liberal Democrat or progressive Tory has reason to reject" them.[8] It is not immediately clear what this objection is. Cohen presumably does not mean simply that the principles do not display sufficient product differentiation. He must mean that they are not radical enough. But the Commission explicitly said that radicalism lay in the understanding and application of these principles: while other parties might affirm them, those parties did not realise how radical the effect would be if the principles were properly and consistently applied. Cohen does not mention this. One explanation is that he cannot accept that the radical application of principles which others might accept could ever be radical enough for the Labour party. The Labour party must not just be radical, but radical in some quite distinctive way. That way, I take it, lies in a notion of community. But, more than that, it must lie in the Labour party's *own distinctive conception of community*, since liberal democrats, again, or not so progressive Conservatives, may be quite keen on community. The Left must want strongly egalitarian community, and it is this, I take it, that Cohen supposes is offered by the manifest tradition of the Labour party, and cravenly or cynically neglected by the Commission.

What is this tradition? Cohen does not actually tell us, but I presume that he has in mind an outlook which combined, as one might say, an experience and a hope: the experience was of a strong sense of community combined with class solidarity, and the hope was that this could be generalised in some way to the whole of society, so that there would be a shared sense of fairness, social humiliation would disappear, and selfish motives would be replaced by altruistic ones. I do not want to deny the existence of such a tradition, or to belittle it. However, there are real and fundamental questions of what this experience was, and how it was related to the hope. Cohen agrees that the social circumstances in which such an outlook existed, to the extent that it did, no longer obtain. This does not just mean that (as Cohen of course also agrees) it is not there to be appealed to. It also means that unless the serious historical questions are answered, of what that outlook was, what socially supported it, and of where it went, we shall not be able to say what the relevant tradition was, or in what form we might now appeal to it.

The Commission's publications prominently featured an historical analysis of the differences between social conditions now and those of fifty years ago. This does not answer these questions about the tradition, but it does bear on them. Cohen does not address this historical analysis, or these questions, at all.

The manifest tradition which he takes for granted involved a whole set of alliances and conjunctures, which were peculiar to their times, and which indeed differed, to some extent, from time to time. In the war, at the high point of the Beveridge spirit, there was perhaps a special combination of a sense of class solidarity with a wider sentiment of national community. This was significantly different from something which had existed earlier and lasted longer, rough coincidence between the interests of the organised working class and the interests, more generally, of the worse-off. The Labour party, like parties of the Left elsewhere, relied on this for a long time, but more recently it has dramatically fallen apart, and to the extent that supporters of the Left go on as though this had not happened, they show less social understanding than Margaret Thatcher did.

Again, and very significantly for the history of the Labour party, there was solidarity within working class communities themselves, which writers such as Raymond Williams celebrated. There was no doubt much to celebrate, balanced as it must be against the deformations that are less remembered now, though some of them, at least, were well rehearsed in those times by liberals and radicals who wanted to change that world. But it is not the fact or the extent of the bad things – the xenophobia, brutality and sexism, the public surveillance – that are the main concern in this argument, but rather the point that the good features just as much as the bad were the product of deprivation. Such communities were complex adaptations to economic and social disadvantage, and were bound to disappear when that disadvantage was alleviated. As Kierkegaard marvellously put it: "Adversity doesn't just knit people together but elicits also that beautiful inner community, as the frost forms patterns on the windowpane which the warmth of the sun then erases."[9]

Cohen does not tell us how to understand the traditions of community, or how to free them from their obvious historical conditions and limitations. Until he does so, we have no reason to think that his appeal to the manifest tradition gives us anything at all except a trip down Memory Lane. He wants us to rely, not just on ideas of equality or, indeed, ideas of community, but on very particular articulations of those values which can supposedly be recovered from the tradition of the Labour party. But unless we understand what has happened to the Labour party, and to the society and the world in which the Labour party has existed, we have no way of knowing what that tradition meant in the past, and hence what it might mean to us today.

Markets and Marx

There are questions, not only about the historical conditions of those earlier hopes, and their practicability today, but about their content. "The immediate motive to productive activity in a market society", Cohen writes,[10] "is typically some mixture of greed and fear", and the only qualification introduced by "typically", a footnote tells us, is that "a sense of service" can exist even in a market society. This extraordinary remark leaves out entirely one of the most significant motives expressed in markets: mutual advantage. This is not simply a theoretical point, but one that has great relevance to a political or social order. If an immigrant to Britain from Pakistan sets up a newsagent or grocery which serves the local customers, it is not obvious to me (nor to him) that either he or his customers are necessarily driven by greed or fear (indeed, in his situation, his business may help to keep away fear). This, and many other such truths, are so obvious, and so spectacularly overlooked by Cohen, that I can only suppose that he has in mind a model of some markets rather than others, in particular of a labour market based on unequal income.

It is still a question, to what extent such a market is driven by greed and fear. It is a further question, whether the fear, at any rate, and at least some manifestations of greed, might not be alleviated by legislation based on the Commission's principles. But this is not a question that Cohen raises, and it is not one that I shall take up. I want to take up, in conclusion, a much more general point about Cohen's outlook. It arises from his remark,[11] that these are not "attractive" motives, and that we would rather do without them if we could. Soon after raising this question, he mentions the name of Marx.

There is a notable paradox in this conjunction, and it tells us something about the assumptions on which Cohen bases his case. Why should anyone suppose that an effective and creative society, not merely in economic terms but more generally, could be based entirely on "attractive" motives? Certainly Marx did not; he was particularly insistent that unattractive motives were necessary to historical advance. Of course, he did think that they would wither away when class conflict was eliminated and history no longer advanced. Cohen, a world expert on Marx, does not need to be told this. But he does need to be asked whether he still accepts the Marxist idea of the end of history. If not, does he accept Marx's view about the world we have, in which history and economic development do still obtain, that it is one in which there cannot simply be attractive motives? If he does accept this view about the world we have, and does not believe in the revolutionary transformation of that world, then perhaps he had better accept the Commission's general definition of the problem of social justice, that aspirations for equality and a sense of community must be applied, by defensible political power, to a world which is significantly driven by other sorts of motivations.

Marxists, as opposed to the Utopian socialists whom they tended to despise, notably believed in two things: the political importance of a sound historical analysis, and a firmly unsentimental picture of what made people act. It is a remarkable dialectical turn by which, in both these respects, it seems to be the Commission rather than Cohen who are in touch with traditions of Marxist socialism.

Endnotes

1.   GA Cohen in this volume p29.

2.   GA Cohen in this volume p39.

3.   *ibid* p39.

4.   Cohen note 30.

5.   Stuart White, in this volume "To satisfy the equal chance condition we must ... consciously regulate the distribution of strategic goods such as income and wealth so as to correct and compensate for these brute luck inequalities." p61.

6.   Stuart White in this volume p69.

7.   Cohen *op cit* p32.

8.   Cohen p33.

9.   Written in 1835: *Papers and Journals: a selection,* translated and edited by Alastair Hannay; Penguin Books, 1996, p39.

10. Cohen p36.

11. Cohen p36.

What do Egalitarians Want?
Stuart White

Introduction

Like many people who first became politically active on the left in the 1980s, I spent a large part of that decade attending a seemingly endless series of meetings and seminars with titles like "rethinking socialism", or even, more bleakly, "socialism: is there a future?" For I had come of age in a decade when, retreating before the increasingly self-confident intellectual and political onslaughts of the New Right, the left (or at least its less blinkered and more rational parts) had begun a process of close self-interrogation and probing, tentative reconstruction that is still far from complete today. At the heart of this process of self-interrogation and reconstruction there were two basic questions to which participants would continually return, and to which they still return today. The first concerned values: how, at the level of principle, do we ("the Left", "socialists") conceive of the good society? What values are distinctive to us and our conception of the good society? The second concerned means: given a proper understanding of our values, how can we effectively implement or advance these values at the institutional level? What is the core institutional apparatus, so to speak, of our good society?

In the British context, the Commission on Social Justice has provided an important focus for this continued process of self-interrogation and reconstruction as we have moved into the 1990s, and debate surrounding the Commission has been framed, once again, by variants of these two basic questions. Thus, at the level of values, the Commission has focused attention on the question: what does a distinctively left, or egalitarian, conception of social justice look like? Following on from this, at the level of means, commentators have asked: do the institutional arrangements and policies advocated in the Commission's final report, *Social Justice: Strategies for National Renewal*, offer any prospect of significant advance from the standpoint of a distinctively egalitarian conception of justice?

These are the two questions that I wish to return to in this essay. I want to explore, at the level of values, what it is that egalitarians want (or ought to want), and, at the level of means, whether the Commission's preferred reform strategy can reasonably be expected to deliver what egalitarians (ought to) want. The answers we give to such questions will determine how we assess the Commission: as marking a genuine, if tentative step on the uncertain path to left renewal, or as merely exemplifying a sad tendency for those on the left passively to adapt their preferences – over institutions and policies, and more fundamentally, over values – to the perceived limits of what the New Right and the new global capitalism have now made possible.[1]

In Part I of this essay, *What do egalitarians want?*, I begin the discussion by setting out the principles which, in my view, lie at the heart of a genuinely egalitarian perspective on social justice. These include *the brute luck principle* (which requires that we correct for or prevent disadvantage attributable to differential "brute luck"); *the fair exchange principle* (which requires that we protect individuals from vulnerability in the market-place, and its potentially exploitative effects); and *the reciprocity principle* (which requires that we prevent economic free-riding). In its first interim report, *The Justice Gap*, the Commission courted controversy amongst political theorists and philosophers by explicitly rejecting one of these principles -the brute luck principle, at least in its simplest and strongest form. In the second half of Part I, I examine the Commission's critique of this egalitarian principle, grounded in the notions of "entitlement" and "desert", and show them to be weak and unpersuasive.

In Part II of the essay, *A Strategy for Equality?*, I argue that the Commission's strategy, centring on what I call endowment egalitarianism and an active welfare state organised on a modernised social insurance basis, is, nevertheless, an ethically attractive one from the standpoint of the principles of egalitarian justice delineated in Part I (notwithstanding the Commission's confused efforts, at the philosophical level, to repudiate the brute luck principle). This claim is subject to some important qualifications, however. Most importantly, I argue that in setting out its strategy, the Commission exaggerates the interdependency between justice and efficiency, and, relatedly, understates the extent to which a strategy for achieving social justice must inevitably rely upon conventional income redistribution, or "Levelling". In addition, I argue that while the Commission tacitly endorses the reciprocity principle, it fails rigorously to pursue some of the "tougher" implications of this principle in the areas of welfare policy and the tax treatment of inheritance. There is, I therefore conclude, much that the egalitarian can and should welcome in the Commission's report, but further development of the Commission's reform strategy, and of its philosophical underpinnings, remain necessary.

Part I: What do Egalitarians Want?

What do egalitarians want? The answer that they want "equality" is, of course, hardly very illuminating by itself since this ideal is so ambiguous and contestable. To be sure, all egalitarians are committed to some basic notion of the equal worth of all persons, and to the view that the major institutions of society and rules of social co-operation must somehow embody this principle of equal worth. But to say this, important as it is, is not to say all that much by way of clarification. Libertarian philosophers, like Robert Nozick, can also plausibly claim that their conception of the just society satisfies this principle, for in their preferred society all persons would at least have equal rights of self-ownership, acquisition and transfer.[2] And surely no one would want to claim that Nozick's libertarianism, which issues, ideally speaking, in a complete endorsement of *laissez-faire*, is a form of egalitarianism.

Three core principles of egalitarian justice

Egalitarian philosophers stake out a distinctive position, however, when they build on the basic principle of equal worth in the following way. If we regard people as having equal moral worth, then, the egalitarian suggests, we ought also to regard them as having a right to something like an equal chance to live a fulfilling life. We may call this the *equal chance condition*. Now, formal equality of opportunity and the absence of discrimination, important as they are, are not enough to satisfy this equal chance condition.[3] Even when there is formal equality of opportunity, some individuals will have significantly lower life-chances, less effective freedom one might say,[4] than others due to differences in skills, handicaps, and holdings of wealth which cannot (always) be attributed to individuals" different choices, but which are simply a matter of differential "brute luck". One person may then have significantly less effective freedom than another through no fault of his/her own. To satisfy the equal chance condition we must, therefore, consciously regulate the distribution of strategic goods such as income and wealth so as to correct and compensate for these brute luck inequalities. We may refer to this, for short, as *the brute luck principle*.[5]

In its simplest and strongest form, the principle can be thought of as calling for the prevention of, or correction/compensation for, any and all brute luck inequality in the key strategic goods which determine prospects for well-being and agency. We may call this the *comprehensive* version of the brute luck principle. Surely what matters most urgently from the moral point of view, however, is that everyone has an equal chance of leading a decent, minimally fulfilling life and, accordingly, that we prevent, or correct/compensate for, brute luck disadvantage in strategic goods insofar as this pushes people below certain *decency thresholds* in their prospects for well-being and agency. This commitment describes what we may term the *threshold* version of the brute luck principle. This version of the principle is perhaps less distinctively egalitarian, but so long as we are willing to set the threshold at a reasonably high level, that is, we have a fairly generous understanding of what a decent life requires, it remains a demanding principle, and in any case, as suggested, one which captures what is morally most urgent in the egalitarian's commitment to prevent or correct/compensate for brute luck inequality.

The concept of brute luck disadvantage does not capture everything that excites egalitarian concern, however. Egalitarians are also concerned to prevent economic exploitation. This latter concern may often overlap with the former, but is not reducible to it.[6] While the concept of exploitation is often appealed to in left-wing literature, it is a concept which is seldom clearly defined. What *is* exploitation? As a very general definition, we can say that to exploit someone is to "take unfair advantage" of that person. But then we have to say something about the exact nature of the unfairness involved here.

Let us start with a stark and simple example. I need a job or I will starve. You are an employer who can offer me a job. I know of no other jobs that are available, but I do know that there are many others who want this job. You take advantage of my (and those other's) desperation to drive a very hard bargain in which I agree to work for you for a very low wage, and in conditions that, while inexpensive to you, are risky for my health. This case roughly describes one sort of exploitation. The essence of the unfairness involved here consists of the way one party takes advantage of the *market vulnerability* of another party to effect a trade of a kind, on terms that the vulnerable party would not consent to were he or she not vulnerable in the relevant way. In this most extreme form, depicted in the foregoing example, market vulnerability arises when: (1) the individual lacks acceptable alternatives to making the exchange in question, an alternative being "unacceptable" if it entails a level of well-being that is both lower than that achieved through the trade, and very low in absolute terms (for example, starvation); and (2) the party with whom he or she is bargaining does not need to make the trade with anything like the same urgency.[7] In capitalist societies, relationships between workers and employers sometimes exhibit vulnerabilities of this kind, and thus, some degree of exploitation in exchange. A second principle of egalitarian justice, the fair exchange principle, states that trades entered into against a background of market vulnerability are unfair, and calls upon public authority to prevent market vulnerability or else to alleviate its exploitative effects. This principle arguably captures some of the moral concerns raised by the Commission in its discussion of the concept of "fair reward".[8]

Consider now another example. There are 1,000 fisherfolk on an island. Their government sends each of them a request for funds to build a lighthouse so as to stop their fishing boats colliding with the shore. 900 of them send funds in, and these are sufficient for the lighthouse to be built. All of the 1,000 island inhabitants then benefit from the lighthouse, including the 100 non-contributors who also wanted the lighthouse built, and were able to contribute to its cost, but who refrained from sending in any funds. This example describes, I think, another kind of exploitation. The non-contributors take unfair advantage of the contributors by "free-riding" on the latter's contributions. Such free-riding is unfair, and therefore exploitative, because the free-rider is trying to enjoy a kind of "objectionably preferential treatment" in access to social goods (to enjoy them without bearing a share of their cost), and thus acts in a way that violates the very principle of equal worth that is foundational to egalitarianism.[9]

The concern to prevent free-riding suggests a third principle of egalitarian justice, which we may term the reciprocity principle. According to this principle, those who willingly accept the economic benefits of social co-operation have a corresponding obligation to make a productive contribution, if so able, to the co-operative community which provides these benefits. Everyone who receives, say, some decent minimum of income, ought to "do his or her bit", within the bounds of his or her ability, in return. Those who do not will be sharing in the economic benefits of social co-operation without bearing their fair share of the cost of producing these benefits, and will thus be living unfairly at the expense of those others who do make such a contribution.[10]

Historically, the reciprocity principle has played an important role in socialist and egalitarian thought. Such a principle can be seen to underlie the Marxist charge that the capitalist robs the worker of labour product, as well as the New Liberal and ethical socialist critique of what R H Tawney called "functionless property" (income entitlements that are divorced from the performance of any productive function).[11] The just society, for Marxists and ethical socialists alike, is one in which all citizens do their productive bit, within the bounds of their ability, in return for the goods and opportunities which the community makes available to them.

So, in answer to the question "What do egalitarians want?", I think we can now answer that egalitarians are centrally committed:

(1) To the prevention or correction of brute luck disadvantage, with special moral urgency attaching to the prevention or correction of absolute or threshold disadvantage.

(2) To the prevention of market vulnerability in the negotiation of the terms and content of market transactions, or, where this is not possible, to the alleviation of the effects of such vulnerability.

(3) To the prevention of economic free-riding – that is, to distributive arrangements that satisfy the reciprocity principle.

Is the reform strategy set out in the Commission's final report consistent with these core commitments? This is the question to which we will shortly turn in Part II. Before doing so, however, I want to take a brief look at one aspect of the Commission's own attempt to set out a working conception of justice: its criticism and rejection of the first of our three core principles – the brute luck principle.

Brute luck, entitlement, and desert

In its first interim report, *The Justice Gap*, the Commission claims that "there is a basic justice in people having some differential reward for their productive activities". Moreover, it claims that unequal rewards for unequal productivities are justified when the differences in productivity are attributable to unequal talent. "[O]utstanding talent should be [specially] rewarded".[12] Now, to the extent that differences in talent reflect differences in natural ability, they are clearly a matter of brute luck, and so this latter claim entails a rejection of the view that any/all brute luck inequality in income (or, more fundamentally, in effective freedom) is unjust. Thus, when, in its final report, the Commission says that "not all inequalities are unjust", this means: "not all inequalities, *including some brute luck inequalities,* are unjust." "Luck is everywhere", remarks the Commission, "and one is entitled to some rewards of luck".[13]

The Commission thus rejects the first of the three principles of egalitarian justice delineated above, the brute luck principle – at least in its simplest and strongest, comprehensive form. It is important to be clear as to what is being asserted here. The Commission does not say that the elimination of brute luck inequalities is *prima facie* desirable, but a goal which must be qualified by respect for other values, such as individual autonomy, which might be compromised were we to try to eliminate all brute luck inequality; nor does the Commission argue that it is a desirable goal whose pursuit, alas, must be qualified by the constraints of economic efficiency. Troublesome value conflicts of this sort can be, and are, avoided by the Commission because it claims that the elimination of brute luck inequality is not even desirable in principle. What arguments does the Commission advance to defend this claim? And how plausible are they?

In what is a frustratingly diffuse and inchoate manner, the Commission attempts to ground its rejection of the brute luck principle in the concepts of "entitlement" and "desert". The document claims, in effect, that some brute luck inequalities, particularly those linked to differential talent, can be just in virtue of the fact that individuals are "entitled" to, or have come to "deserve", special rewards.[14]

Now the appeal to "entitlement" is question-begging. To say that someone is entitled to something is merely to say that she has a morally legitimate claim to that thing which others are accordingly obliged to respect. But to say this is to leave wide open the question of the *moral grounds* in virtue of which she may legitimately press this claim. The bare notion of entitlement needs to be filled out by· reference to some more fundamental concept, such as need, equal consideration, due process, or possibly desert, which provides the moral grounds of the supposed entitlement. The disagreement between the egalitarian and the anti-egalitarian is not about whether or not, or to what extent, the claims of entitlement should trump those of equality, but rather, about what, morally speaking, establishes an entitlement in the first place. One cannot therefore just assert that people are entitled to things (eg, "one is entitled to some rewards of luck"),[15] and then pit entitlement against the claims of equality in the manner supposed in *The Justice Gap;* rather, one must show that there is some other, deeper moral consideration which establishes such an entitlement, a consideration strong enough to defeat the counter-claims of equality.

Is "desert" perhaps one such consideration? More specifically, can we use the notion of desert to defend higher incomes for more productive workers, when their superior productivity is attributable, say, to differential natural talent? To assess the plausibility of desert claims in this kind of case, it may help to consider the following example. Albert and Barbara work for the same length of time producing widgets, and at the same intensity, but Albert produces more widgets just because he happens to have been gifted by nature with better widget-making skills (say, especially dextrous hands). Is Albert entitled, on grounds of desert, to a higher income?

In thinking about our answer to this question it may help to consider another. What if the difference in output between Albert and Barbara stems not from Albert's natural gift for widget-making, but from the fact that when they arrived at the factory in the morning they were each randomly assigned to a widget-making machine, and Albert's machine just happened to be more efficient than Barbara's? Would Albert then deserve a higher income in virtue of his higher productivity? It is surely implausible to say in this second case that Albert is deserving of higher reward in virtue of his higher productivity. But, one might then ask, how is this case significantly different from our first case? In both cases Albert himself is in no way responsible for that which explains his superior productivity; in both cases, he benefits from some sort of "mechanical good fortune" – in one case in the form of being endowed that particular morning with a superior widget-making machine, and, in the other case, by being endowed with, as it were, a superior widget-making body (especially dextrous hands). How can the *particular form* of the mechanical good fortune he enjoys make a moral difference? If he is undeserving of higher reward in the machine case, surely he cannot be any more deserving in the original, dextrous hands case.

But now consider another case. There are two pianists, Paula and Quentin. They practice equally hard, but, come the big night of the grand performance, Paula performs much better simply because she has more innate ability than Quentin. This is reflected in the applause each receives. While Quentin is politely clapped for a few minutes, Paula receives a prolonged standing ovation. It would surely be rather odd for Quentin to object that Paula did not deserve the extra applause because the superiority of her performance was entirely attributable to greater innate ability for which she herself is in no way responsible. This suggests that one person can reasonably be said to be more deserving than another in virtue of a superior performance *even where the superiority in performance is attributable to a brute luck inequality in natural ability.*

Having said that, however, it does not follow that what the superior pianist deserves is a *higher income.* What Paula arguably deserves is precisely what she got – extra applause, praise, esteem. Ditto for popular opera singers, rock stars, popular comedians, and sporting legends. Why presume that the appropriate currency for rewarding desert in such cases is (higher) income? In short, while this example shows that desert claims based on a superiority in performance, where the superiority is attributable to a brute luck inequality in talent or ability, are by no means morally unintelligible, we can still question the appropriateness of acknowledging the desert claim by paying the superior performer a higher income.

We probably feel more confident in saying that one person deserves a higher income than another when one person is more productive because she has put in more effort, rather than merely because she just happens to be naturally more talented. But then effort is something which we tend to think of, in most cases, and to some extent, as being under the control of the individual, so that effort-based inequalities in income will not strike us in general as being clearly attributable to differential brute luck. And in those cases where differences in effort can be attributed to differential brute luck, I am not sure we feel as confident in saying that higher effort is deserving of higher reward. Imagine, for example, that one person has just entered work after a prolonged period of involuntary unemployment which has left him physically weaker than his co-workers. Because of this he is unable to work as hard as they do. Do we feel confident in saying that the debilitated worker deserves a lower income than his co-workers because he puts in less effort? One can readily imagine the worker staring at his wage packet, acknowledging the difference between his pay and that of his co-workers, and, in the light of the series of uncontrollable misfortunes which explains his situation, saying: "What have I done to *deserve* this? It's not as if its *my fault* that I can't work as hard as the others at the moment." I contend, then, that effort-based inequalities in material reward either do not conflict with the brute luck principle, or that where they do, we feel less confident that the relevant inequalities in reward are genuinely deserved.

In short, the brute luck principle can accommodate our strongest intuitions about desert because it allows for inequalities attributable to choice rather than brute luck; and where the putative claims of desert do conflict with the principle, our intuitions about desert as a basis for differential reward are then probably all the weaker. Desert, therefore, does not provide a very persuasive basis on which to reject the brute luck principle. And the Commission's attempt to repudiate the principle by appeal to the notions of entitlement and desert must consequently be regarded as unpersuasive.

However, as I suggested above, the morally urgent consideration is not so much strict equality of life-chances, but ensuring that everyone has an equal chance to live a minimally decent, fulfilling life. The primary concern of the egalitarian, in other words, is to ensure that individuals do not fall below certain decency thresholds through no fault of their own. Prevention or correction for brute luck inequalities over and above such thresholds, even if it remains *prima facie* desirable, is just not as important. Now, for all its talk of entitlement and desert, the Commission does not retreat from this threshold version of the brute luck principle. Clear evidence for this is provided by the second of its "four key ideas", introduced in *The Justice Gap*, which states that "all citizens are entitled ... to be able to meet their basic needs ... " The Commission does not reject the demands of the brute luck principle, then, at the point where the egalitarian believes they have most force.

Secondly, whatever the Commission's philosophical position regarding the brute luck principle, it is conceivable that the Commission's reform strategy may still go some considerable way towards reducing the extent of brute luck inequality in income (and effective freedom) above and beyond just getting everyone up to the aforementioned decency threshold. The third of the Commission's four key ideas calls for the "widest possible access to opportunities and life-chances", and, as I shall explain below, the policies set out by the Commission to achieve this can reasonably be expected to reduce, in a well-targeted manner, the general extent of brute luck income inequality. It is possible, then, that a supporter of the brute luck principle, even in its strong form, may still find much to support in the Commission's reform strategy, and could quite consistently invoke the principle in defence of these elements of the strategy, even if the Commission itself was loathe to do so.

To pursue this point we must take a closer look at the content of the reform strategy set out by the Commission. It is to this task that we now turn.

Part II: A Strategy for Equality?

Beneath the detail of the Commission's final report, lie three core organising ideas: that justice is to be promoted through a more equal distribution of productive endowments, such as skills, and not only through conventional income redistribution; that justice and efficiency are interdependent values; and that, in a just and cohesive society, rights are balanced by responsibilities. Examining each of these ideas in turn, I shall explore, in Part II of this essay, the consistency of the Commission's reform strategy with the egalitarian principles delineated in Part I.

The core of the Commission's strategy: endowment egalitarianism

How can we hope to reduce inequality in life-chances in a market economy? Firstly, we can simply try to redistribute incomes while taking background inequalities in the distribution of productive endowments – capital and skills – as given. Alternatively, we can try to equalise the background distribution of productive endowments itself so that market interaction leads to a greater initial equality of income, lessening the need for subsequent redistribution.

The reform strategy set out in the Commission's final report places a strong emphasis on the second of these strategies, the strategy of what we may term *endowment egalitarianism*. As the

Commission puts it in *The Justice Gap:* " ... the aims of social justice are served not only by redistribution, by bringing resources after the event to people who have done badly. Social justice requires as well that structures should be adapted and influenced in ways that can give people a better chance in the first place".[16] This endowment egalitarianism underlies the central strategic recommendation of the report which is to increase the access which the average citizen has to education and training, in order to raise the skill level of the workforce as a whole, with a special emphasis on raising the skill level of those most lacking in skills. To this end, the report advocates the establishment of a national Learning Bank, at which each citizen will have an Individual Learning Account, financed from a combination of public and private sources, providing access to the equivalent of three years full-time education (pp.141-147).[17] To address the skill deficiencies of those groups most disadvantaged in the labour market, the report also recommends the establishment of a Jobs, Education and Training (JET) programme specifically targeted on the long-term unemployed and single parents in receipt of welfare benefits (pp.170-182).

This endowment egalitarian approach is, I think, eminently sensible and ethically attractive for a number of reasons of which I will note three here.

The first reason, strongly emphasised in the report itself, is that it may well make for an improved overall trade-off between justice and efficiency. A radical levelling-up of access to education and training will not only help to reduce inequality, but, as I will explain in a moment, can also be expected to improve overall economic performance.

A second possible advantage lies in the potential effect of the endowment egalitarian approach on market vulnerability. Some people enter the market-place with very minimal productive endowments, including skills. This limits their market opportunities, increasing the risk of vulnerability and exploitation. Workers who are more broadly and highly skilled are likely to have correspondingly wider market options, and are therefore less likely to suffer market vulnerability and exploitation – potentially a big plus from the standpoint of the fair exchange principle.

The third possible advantage of endowment egalitarianism is that its inclusion in any egalitarian strategy will almost certainly make for a better "targeted" approach to the reduction of brute luck inequality than a single-minded reliance on conventional income redistribution. In the real world, income inequalities will usually reflect a complex mixture of brute luck and choice. As a result, there will be an enormous problem in targeting income redistribution through the tax-transfer system so that it corrects for unjust brute luck inequalities, while preserving legitimate choice-based inequalities. It would be much better if we could find some way of *preventing* the emergence of brute luck inequalities in the first place, rather than relying on a subsequent redistribution of incomes to *correct* them after the fact. And this immediately points us in the direction of addressing the background distribution of productive endowments, such as skills, which are such an important determinant of citizens initial opportunities to acquire income and wealth. By adopting an endowment egalitarian approach we can make these opportunities more equal, and so reduce the extent to which the material inequalities subsequently thrown up in the market are a reflection of differential brute luck rather than choice; this, in turn, will reduce our need to rely on the blunt instrument of conventional income redistribution to minimise the extent of unjust, brute luck inequality.

The endowment egalitarian approach has special relevance for a country like the UK which has witnessed a significant increase in income inequality in the last fifteen years driven, to a considerable extent, by increased earnings inequality and high levels of unemployment.[18] The increase in earnings inequality has occurred in large part due a relative demand shift away from unskilled to skilled labour, while research indicates that lack of skills in the workforce has also been an important factor behind high levels of unemployment.[19] In both cases, the solution would therefore necessarily seem to involve more education and training, focusing especially on those currently most lacking in skills; and such measures are, as we have seen, at the very heart of the endowment egalitarian approach.

Having made these points, however, we must also acknowledge the limits of endowment egalitarianism. We should not naively suppose that an endowment egalitarian approach will completely prevent the emergence of brute luck income inequality or market vulnerability. Underlying differences in natural ability, and, therefore, market opportunity, will always remain, and even if each citizen had identical endowments of skills and other productive assets, some citizens would still end up badly off through no fault of their own and/or in a position of market vulnerability. As I shall illustrate below, there are large constituencies of currently needy people for whom such a strategy has little or no relevance, simply because they are, due to age or infirmity, non-productive members of society. Conventional income redistribution will therefore still have an important role to play in correcting for brute luck disadvantage and alleviating market vulnerability.

Does the Commission acknowledge this? At one level, the answer must be "yes". The second major element in the Commission's reform strategy is an "intelligent welfare state", organised on a modernised social insurance basis, which can be expected to satisfy the demands of at least the threshold version of the brute luck principle and, in the process, to alleviate the pressure felt by unfortunate individuals to enter into exploitative, "desperate trades". As I shall shortly explain, however, I think the Commission can nevertheless be faulted for the importance of conventional redistribution – or, more specifically, for adopting a rhetoric, centring on a simplistic contrast between "Levellers" and "Investors", that serves to obscure it.

A supply-side marriage of justice and efficiency?

As said, one argument in favour of the report's endowment egalitarian approach is that it apparently holds out the prospect of marrying the values of justice and efficiency.[20] The Commission's report is, to put it mildly, enthralled with this prospect. Its constant refrain is that the two values go together. Thus we are told: " ... the economic success of our country requires a greater measure of social justice" (p.18); "there will be no solid economic success without more social justice" (p.18); "social justice is not simply a moral ideal but an economic necessity" (p.19). In short: "[Britain] must be both fairer and more successful if it is to be either ... it is a constant theme of this report that there is not an opposition between [social justice and economic efficiency]. On the contrary, each demands the other" (p.17).[21]

The central, underlying thought here is that, for countries like Britain, the health of the whole economy depends on having a competitive trade sector, and that the most promising product market strategy for firms in this sector to adopt is not the traditional strategy of competing in the production of standardised goods on the basis of cost alone, but that of competing in the production of more complex, differentiated goods, where quality matters as well as price (pp.99-102). However, successful adoption of this competitive strategy requires a broadly and highly skilled workforce (which the free-market cannot be relied upon to provide). Justice-promoting policies such as the Learning Bank and the JET programme will help to produce a workforce with the requisite level of skill, and can thus be expected to improve economic competitiveness and performance even as they reduce brute luck inequality and market exploitation.[22] This, I think, is the main line of argument underlying the report's attempt to marry the values of justice and efficiency.

Now the report is almost certainly right to point to this area of interdependency between justice and efficiency. Nevertheless, the Commission almost certainly exaggerates the degree to which the two values are mutually supportive, and, as a result, fails sufficiently to affirm the importance of justice as a value in its own right – and the continuing importance of conventional income redistribution as a necessary complement to endowment egalitarianism.

The limits of endowment egalitarianism

Some individuals in our society are never going to be significant economic contributors due to mental or physical disabilities they suffer. Since, in general, they suffer these disabilities as a matter of brute luck, justice, as the egalitarian conceives it, requires that the community support these individuals, paying them sufficient benefits to cover their needs and to help compensate for their disabilities. There is, however, absolutely no way in which these payments can be meaningfully said to contribute to improving the economy's competitive strength. The payments in question are pure transfers and cannot be characterised as "investment" expenditures in any meaningful sense. The same could be said, for instance, of transfers to the needy and non-productive elderly. If anything, such transfers probably detract from the economy's competitive strength, for an opportunity cost of making these payments is higher expenditure on education and training, or on investment on infrastructure, either of which would (according to the Commission's analysis) improve competitiveness.

Simple examples such as these suggest that, to some extent, the values of social justice and economic efficiency can and do conflict. While some theorists of the New Right may have been too simplistic in presenting the two values as necessarily always in conflict, the Commission on Social Justice proceeds to commit the inverse fallacy of presenting them as completely reconcilable ("it is a constant theme of this report that there is not an opposition between [them]"). The prosaic truth of the matter is that in some areas the two values are mutually supportive, and that in others they are antagonistic. In certain, specific policy areas, we do have to face up to an ugly trade-off between them, and it is either morally or economically naive to think otherwise.

The inevitability of "levelling"

Now, precisely because in certain respects the pursuit of justice will compromise economic efficiency, it is very important for those who value social justice to continue to affirm the claims of justice independently of its contribution to efficiency. Rather than doing this, however, the Commission proceeds to articulate its conception of a just society in a language that trades very heavily on the supposed interdependency between the two values. Thus, most notably, its vision of a just society is summarised as a vision of an "Investor's Britain", in contrast to the primitive redistribution principle of a so-called "Leveller's Britain". But as we have seen, not every policy which justice demands can be felicitously described as a type of investment policy; some of these policies *will* be purely and simply a matter of "levelling". The political danger in the Commission's position, and the rhetoric through which it is expressed, is that if one tries to build support for justice-promoting policies solely by reference to their contribution to economic efficiency, people may be less ready to respond to the claims of social justice when, as may often happen, justice conflicts with efficiency. The intellectual danger is that we may come to overstate the case for the endowment egalitarian approach, and understate the inevitable need for straightforward income redistribution in pursuing social justice.

The role of reciprocity in the Commission's strategy

The Commission's final report speaks frequently of its "ambition of creating a "something for something" society ... where rights are matched by responsibilities" (p.362). In this way, the report tacitly endorses the third principle of egalitarian justice introduced in Part I, the reciprocity principle.

Concretely, the Commission's endorsement of this principle is most evident in its proposals for the construction of an "intelligent welfare state". The key proposal here is for a system of "modernised social insurance", the creation of which would involve expanding the categories of workers covered by the social insurance system, and the introduction of a range of new social insurance benefits to cover various contingencies which are ignored by the present system, such as a part-time employment benefit, and a benefit to cover periods of parental leave (pp.227-245). The report defends the social insurance approach on the grounds that it "balances rights with responsibilities" (p.231), and thus expresses "an ethic of mutuality which is essential if we are to create a better community" (p.232). The appeal to reciprocity also underpins the report's proposal for a new "Citizens' Service", a voluntary community service scheme in which young people, especially school-leavers, would perform various sorts of community work, in areas such as conservation and caring services, and, in return, would receive credits to help finance higher education or training (pp.361-369).

However, having tacitly endorsed and appealed to the reciprocity principle, the Commission is less than resolute in pursuing some of its implications. This is most evident in its discussion of "Citizen's Income", and, to a lesser extent, in its treatment of inheritance taxation.

Advocates of Citizen's Income argue that each citizen should receive as of right a substantial cash income, without a "means-test", and which is not conditional on any past, present, or future productive contribution. This is a proposal for a right which is not balanced by a corresponding contributive responsibility. It is therefore vulnerable to the objection that it would enable citizens to free-ride on, and so exploit, fellow citizens who do make the productive contribution required by the reciprocity principle. In the language of Tawney, a citizen's income is a species of functionless property, and as such is immoral. The Commission's final report comments on the proposal as follows:

> [The introduction of a sizeable Citizen's Income] would have to be backed by a broad-based consensus, of which there is, as yet, no sign. In a society with a strong work ethic many people would oppose, as "giving something for nothing", a scheme deliberately designed to offer unconditional benefits to all. Citizen's Income does not require any act of citizenship; it would be paid regardless of whether someone was in a job or looking for one, caring for children or other dependents, engaged in voluntary work or not (p.262).

I sense some prevarication here as to exactly what the Commission thinks the problem with Citizen's Income is. The final sentence seems to endorse the principled, reciprocity-based objection described above. But in the preceding two sentences the problem seems to be not that a Citizen's Income, for reciprocity-based reasons, is unjust, but rather that many would, alas, just happen to *perceive* it as unjust. It is as if the report cannot decide whether the problem is merely one of public image and political feasibility, as suggested in the first two sentences, or whether there is really is also a genuine ethical objection to the proposal – an objection which would make it undesirable to introduce a Citizen's Income even if it were politically feasible, indeed, which would require us to actively struggle against the emergence of the "broad-based consensus" which is the precondition of its political feasibility. The

Commission cannot bring itself to grasp the nettle and say unequivocally that a Citizen's Income is *prima facie* undesirable on reciprocity-based grounds.[23]

A consistent application of the reciprocity principle would also almost certainly require the heavy taxation of inheritance (plus gifts and bequests) in order to prevent economic free-riding by an "overclass" of citizens who have inherited enough wealth to evade the contributive responsibilities which other, less fortunate citizens have to bear if they wish to enjoy a reasonable level of income. Viewed in this light, the Commission's treatment of inheritance taxation is also disappointing. The final report does advocate a "fairer" system of inheritance taxation, but the recommendation is hidden away towards the back of the report (pp.390-391), and is left rather undeveloped. Crucially, nothing is said about the kind of rates at which wealth transfers should be taxed. The basic legitimacy of inheritance taxation should be more strongly asserted and the relevant policy recommendation should be given proportionately greater prominence and developed in more detail. Heavier taxation of inheritance would cohere neatly, of course, with the underlying endowment egalitarian strategy presented in the report. The connection between the two could perhaps be made more explicit by linking steeper inheritance taxation with the funding of the Learning Bank and/or the JET programme which the report recommends.[24]

Conclusions

Our two questions have been: what do egalitarians want? And: will the reform strategy set out in the final report of the Commission on Social Justice give them what they want?

In response to the first question, I have argued that a society satisfying the brute luck, fair exchange, and reciprocity principles set out in Part I of the essay is essentially what an egalitarian wants. The Commission on Social Justice itself rejected the first of these principles, in its simplest and strongest form, but we have seen that its grounds for doing so were unpersuasive (and it did effectively endorse the principle in its weaker, threshold form which captures what matters most to the egalitarian).

Turning to the second question, I have argued: (1) that the main elements of the Commission's reform strategy are endowment egalitarianism (which focuses on widening access to productive endowments, such as skills), supplemented by an active, redistributive welfare state providing income maintenance on a modernised social insurance basis; (2) that endowment egalitarianism can be expected to reduce the tendency of the market to throw up brute luck inequalities in income, and to promote conditions for fair(er) exchange; (3) that the active welfare state advocated by the Commission can be expected to correct for the more alarming cases of brute luck disadvantage and/or market vulnerability which are likely to arise even when the background distribution of productive endowments has been made more equal than at present; and (4) that the systems of entitlement to welfare, and to education and training, proposed by the Commission are broadly consistent with our third principle of egalitarian justice, the reciprocity principle.

On the other hand, I have argued: (5) that the Commission exaggerates the interdependency of justice and efficiency and, relatedly, understates, though clearly it does not straightforwardly deny, the inevitable importance of conventional income redistribution – or "Levelling" – to the attainment of egalitarian objectives; and (6) that although the Commission tacitly endorses the reciprocity principle, it backs away from some of the "tougher" policy implications of the principle in relation to welfare provision and the tax treatment of inheritance.

In conclusion, therefore, I think that if we are prepared to state more clearly the continuing importance of conventional income redistribution (discarding the Commission's rhetorical contrast between "Investors" and "Levellers'), and to develop further the Commission's policy proposals in certain areas (such as inheritance taxation), then we will have a strategy, based on the Commission's report, that can reasonably be expected to satisfy at least the most morally urgent demands of the brute luck, fair exchange, and reciprocity principles. On this qualified basis, I would argue, therefore, that the Commission's report does represent a useful, though limited, contribution to the task of reconstructing and renewing the egalitarian project.

Endnotes

1. On the danger of adaptive preference formation in the present conjuncture, see G A Cohen (1995) "The Future of a Disillusion", in his *Self-Ownership, Freedom, and Equality*, Cambridge: Cambridge University Press, pp.245-265, especially pp.254-264.

2. Robert Nozick (1974) *Anarchy, State, and Utopia*, Oxford: Basil Blackwell.

3. For purposes of this essay, I take it as self-evident that prevention of discrimination is central to the egalitarian project; and I do not think there can be much doubt that the Commission acknowledges this and proposes appropriate policies. See, in particular, Commission on Social Justice (1994) *Social Justice: Strategies for National Renewal*, London: Vintage, pp.51-52, 194-197.

4. By effective freedom I mean the individual's capability for well-being and agency, grounded in his/her command over strategic goods, such as income, wealth, and basic capacities such as sight, mobility, etc., that have value for well-being and agency across a wide range of conceptions of the good.

5. See G A Cohen "On the Currency of Egalitarian Justice", *Ethics* 99, 1989, pp.906-944.

6. I could, for instance, find myself vulnerable to exploitation as a result of factors that are not a matter of bad brute luck, but a result of my own choices (for example, losing all my resources in a bet to which I gave my fully-informed consent). But the fact that bad brute luck is not part of the causal story which leads to this situation of vulnerability does not necessarily mean there is no exploitation if and when some better placed individual tries to take advantage of it.

7. My characterization of (acute) market vulnerability in terms of the non-availability of acceptable alternatives is derived from G A Cohen's discussion of coerced exchange in "Are Disadvantaged Workers Who Take Hazardous Jobs, Forced to Take Hazardous Jobs?", in his *History, Labour, and Freedom*, Oxford: Oxford University Press, 1987, pp.239-254. But see also R E Goodin (1985) *Protecting the Vulnerable: A Reanalysis of our Social Responsibilities*, Chicago: University of Chicago, pp.195-196.

8. See *The Justice Gap*, pp.15-16.

9. See Garrett Cullity "Moral Free-Riding", *Philosophy and Public Affairs* 24, 1995, pp.3-34, especially pp.22-23.

10. Note that our conception of what counts as a productive contribution in satisfaction of the principle need not be restricted to formal paid employment, but may be expanded to incorporate at least some forms of care work that, at present, typically go unpaid.

11. See R H Tawney (1921) *The Acquisitive Society*, London: Bell, [1945].

12. *The Justice Gap*, p.13. Similarly, *The Justice Gap* claims that " ... one is entitled to some rewards from the product of one's efforts and talents" (p.14), and comments that "rewards in a market economy [may not be] fair, because they are not ... determined by such things as talent, effort, and the person's contribution to the enterprise ... " (p.15), implying that rewards which do reflect differential talent are (or at least can be) fair.

13. *The Justice Gap*, p.13.

14. See especially the section headed "Entitlement and Desert" on pp.12-14 of *The Justice Gap*.

15. *The Justice Gap*, p.13.

16. See *The Justice Gap*, p.11.

17. All page references in the main text are to the Commission's final report, *Social Justice: Strategies for National Renewal*.

18. See Joseph Rowntree Foundation, (1995) *Inquiry into Income and Wealth*, York, Volume 1, especially pp.12-23. These developments are important in explaining the growth in the inequality of original incomes; changes in the tax-benefit system over the same period have meant that this has been mirrored by a similar rate of growth of inequality in final incomes.

19. For a review of recent research on the causes of increased earnings inequality and unemployment, including the crucial role played by the level and distribution of workforce skills, see A Glyn (1995) "The Assessment: Unemployment and Inequality", *Oxford Review of Economic Policy*, 11 (1), pp.1-25.

20. I borrow the marital metaphor from Philippe Van Parijs' paper, "The Second Marriage of Justice and Efficiency", *Journal of Social Policy* 19, 1990, pp.1-25. Note also that I am using the word "efficiency" here in a loose sense to refer to good economic performance as measured by levels of productivity, output, and rates of growth.

21. See also *The Justice Gap*, p.2, and *Social Justice in a Changing World* (London: Institute for Public Policy Research, 1993), p.3.

22. Here the report seems indebted to the kind of analysis set out in J Rogers and W Streeck, "Productive Solidarities: Economic Strategy and Left Politics", in D Miliband, (ed) (1994), *Reinventing the Left*, Cambridge: Polity Press, pp.128-145. See also D Finegold and D Soskice (1988), "The Failure of Training in Britain: Analysis and Prescription", in *Oxford Review of Economic Policy* 4 (3), pp.21-53, and for more recent relevant empirical and policy-oriented work, A Booth and D Snower (eds) (1996) *Acquiring Skills*, Cambridge: Cambridge University Press.

23. Since it is only fair to insist on satisfaction of the reciprocity principle if there are sufficient opportunities for citizens to do so, it would arguably become unfair to continue to affirm the principle were we unable to return to full employment (in an appropriately modernised sense). The case for citizen's income would then be correspondingly stronger. I therefore think the Commission is right to hold out the possibility (on p.263) that if labour market conditions turn out to be worse than expected in future, we should reconsider the case for citizen's income. Note also that the modest "participation income" which the report recommends as a supplement to social insurance benefits (pp.264-265) is not subject to the reciprocity objection precisely because it is conditional, in the case of the able-bodied, on some form of productive contribution, though not necessarily on paid work.

24. A similar suggestion is to use the funds from inheritance taxation gradually to build up a public portfolio of assets, or "community" fund", the dividends from which could then be used to finance increased spending in areas like education and training or health-care. See G Holtham, "A community fund could save social democracy", *The Independent*, April 18, 1995.

What Kind of Equality Should the Left Pursue?[1]

David Miller

The question of equality continues to cause heated controversy among politicians and intellectuals of the Left: witness the recent sharp exchange between Roy Hattersley and Gordon Brown in the pages of *The Guardian*.[2] Hattersley, in his lately assumed role of defender of the Tawneyite socialist faith, argued for equality of outcome as the principle that a Labour government should use to judge every policy proposal; Brown, perhaps the leading intellectual architect of New Labour, claimed that equality of outcome was both unfair and unrealisable, and that a Labour government should instead commit itself to a maximalist version of equality of opportunity. And indeed this is very often the form that the debate over equality takes. Should we be aiming to create a society in which outcomes are equalised – in which everyone gets an equal share of resources, or income, or material benefits of other kinds – or should we recognise that material equality is an impossible dream, and aim instead for a society in which each person gets an equal opportunity to strive for unequal advantages – more education, better jobs, higher incomes?

I want to suggest in this essay that there is a third kind of equality that gets overlooked in this debate, despite the fact that it has inspired generations of democratic socialists and social democrats: this is *social equality* or *equality of status,* by which I mean the idea of a society in which people regard and treat one another as equals, and together form a single community without divisions of social class. This may appear to be a less tangible ideal either than Hattersley's equality of outcome or Brown's equality of opportunity, but I shall try to show in the course of the essay that it can guide our thinking about policy issues in a quite distinctive way. I go along with Brown when he says that material equality of outcome is both unattainable and unjust, but I am concerned that a society guided solely by the principle of equality of opportunity – even in the generous, life-long version that Brown defends – might still be one in which the gap between the successful and the unsuccessful, the qualified and the unqualified, the rich and the poor, was of a size that created sharp class divisions, even within a single generation. We would then have a class-divided meritocracy, better than a society in which class position is largely inherited, but still not a community in which each citizen has an equal standing and there are no hierarchical barriers to friendship and solidarity. I don't, therefore, regard social equality as a value that *replaces* equality of opportunity but as one that stands alongside it to correct its elitist tendencies.

In order to get to closer grips with the question, I want to begin with the work of the Commission on Social Justice, and in particular with the principles of justice that formed the philosophical basis of the Commission's Report. These were summarised in the following four propositions:

(1) The foundation of a free society is the equal worth of all citizens.
(2) Everyone is entitled, as a right of citizenship, to be able to meet their basic needs.
(3) The right to self-respect and personal autonomy demands the widest possible spread of opportunities.
(4) Not all inequalities are unjust, but unjust inequalities should be reduced and where possible eliminated.[3]

A noteworthy feature of these four principles is that they include no commitment to equality per se: *unjust* inequalities are condemned, certainly, but as the fourth principle makes plain, the Commission's view was that some inequalities were just, in particular those corresponding to differences in desert and entitlement. This omission provoked a heated attack by Jerry Cohen in the article reproduced in this volume. Linking together the values of community and equality, he argued that these were the only values which "the Left affirmed as a matter of principle and which the Centre and Right reject as a matter of principle".[4] If these values were abandoned, he claimed, there would be nothing distinctively socialist remaining to distinguish the Labour party from centrist parties like the Liberal Democrats. The Commission's report constituted just such an abandonment, with its embrace of the market signalling the end of the traditional socialist commitment to community, and its principles of justice – particularly its defence of inequalities on grounds of desert and entitlement -signalling the end of the quest for equality. According to Cohen, the principle of equality that socialists have embraced and should embrace "says that the amount of amenity and burden in one person's life should be roughly comparable to that in any other's".[5] Socialists, in other words, must believe in material equality, whereas the Commission's report advocates only the reduction and possible elimination of unjust inequalities, in a context which makes it clear that just inequalities are both conceptually and morally admissible.

Although my thinking about social justice is closely in line with that contained in the Commission's report, I agree with Cohen that there is something more to be said about equality that the Commission does not say and that needs to be set alongside the four principles of social justice that head the Report. But I do not think that Cohen's principle is the one that we should embrace, nor do I think that he is correct to say that equality as a principle is exclusively the property of socialists and the Left. Let me begin with a couple of remarks on this second question.

It is far from evident that equality can be used as a litmus test to mark socialism off from rival political ideologies such as conservatism and liberalism. It is true that conservatives very often disparage equality: they are the ones who write books with titles like *Against Equality*.[6] Nevertheless, these same conservatives quickly make it clear that they are not against equality in all its forms. The conservative rhetorical strategy is to declare in favour of certain limited equalities – equality before the law, equality of opportunity, both narrowly interpreted – and then to denounce anything beyond this as "levelling down" – the equality that says that everyone should have the same incomes, live in the same size houses, be educated in identical schools. And this strategy may be effective, to the extent that once conservatives have picked up what sound like the more appealing principles of equality, there may seem to be nothing left that socialists should want to cling on to.

As for liberals, it is a well known fact about contemporary

liberal philosophy that it has moved the principle of equality to centre stage. A recent authoritative text on political philosophy presents a range of recent liberal thinkers as offering rival articulations of a shared underlying concern that people should be treated as equals.[7] The case of Ronald Dworkin is illuminating here. Dworkin writes as a critic of socialism, yet his liberalism has as its core principle a version of egalitarianism that Dworkin calls "equality of resources".[8] Now admittedly this is not precisely the same principle of equality as the one that Cohen recommends to his fellow socialists, but it appears to be its near neighbour. The dispute between Cohen and Dworkin over "equality of resources" *vs.* "equality of amenity and burden" looks like a case of philosophical fine-tuning. Something is clearly amiss if the social democrat Dworkin can express his central principle in terms of the value which Cohen claims is distinctively and uniquely socialist.

So perhaps what distinguishes socialists from conservatives and liberals is not that they believe in equality while the others don't, but that they give equality a higher priority, or have a better grasp of what it actually takes to implement a principle like equality of opportunity. This last is certainly true: both the Commission's Report and Brown's article in *The Guardian* referred to above, reveal a much more thoroughgoing commitment to equalising opportunities than anything a conservative might support. But this is not the same as saying that there is a principle – equality – which uniquely serves to separate socialists from their ideological opponents.

So let me turn now to the principle of equality itself, in something like the version favoured by Cohen. It suffers from what we might call the Two Bears problem: the porridge is either too hot or too cold. The egalitarian begins with a principle that is very strong and has radical implications: for instance, that everyone should enjoy the same level of resources unless they have special needs or handicaps which entitle them to extra ones. A critic then points out that to pursue such a principle consistently would mean, among other things, rejecting the system of material incentives that makes a market economy possible; forbidding voluntary gifts that disrupted equality, for instance buying Grandma a once-in-a-lifetime Mediterranean cruise; preferring equal poverty to unequal affluence;

and so on. Faced with this barrage of criticisms, our egalitarian then conducts a strategic retreat which looks increasingly like a rout. Two avenues of retreat are especially popular. One consists in saying that equality should be treated only as a *baseline* from which improvements can be made provided everybody benefits. This lead naturally to John Rawls' difference principle, which says that inequalities should be arranged to maximise the share of advantages enjoyed by the least well-off.[9] But this now makes the degree of equality or inequality that counts as just depend entirely on empirical claims about the way in which markets operate, about the size of the incentives that are needed to make entrepreneurial types maximally productive, and so on. If the Thatcherite claim that deregulating the market and privatising the welfare state would in the long run maximise the economic prospects of the worst-off could be shown to be true, then these policies would be chosen by the Rawlsian difference principle. The porridge has gone from being too hot to being decidedly chilly.

The other avenue of retreat consists in saying that material equality is what *justice* requires, but that this value has to be traded off against considerations of efficiency, personal liberty and the like. Economic incentives, for instance, can never be just, but they may be justified on the grounds that they improve productivity and so raise the average standard of living. Now in general there is nothing objectionable in the idea that sometimes we have to sacrifice justice for the sake of other values. Only a fanatic takes the slogan "Let Justice be done though the Heavens fall" literally. But the picture that supports this is one of justice governing most of our transactions and practices from day to day, but then having to be set aside in certain extreme circumstances. Thus one of our basic principles is that no one should be imprisoned without a fair trial, and we hope and expect that this should be adhered to strictly in all normal cases; but if we are realists we should admit that there are conceivable circumstances in which something like internment is necessary to protect civil order. This is unjust – people are held in captivity without a proper chance to prove their innocence – but if the alternative really is going to be political violence that will leave its victims dead on the streets, then we say that justice must yield, temporarily, to the general welfare of society.

However the picture painted by our retreating egalitarian is not like that. He wants to say that justice demands equality of material treatment, but that for reasons of expediency, justice has to be set aside, systematically and for as far ahead as we can see, to allow incentives to operate, voluntary exchange and gift-giving to occur, and so forth. Wearing his realist's hat, the egalitarian comes to acquiesce in a social system that routinely flouts justice as he sees it, so that justice becomes little more than a utopian aspiration, something we might aspire to if citizens could transform their day-to-day motivations from self-interest into a wish to serve their fellows. But this surely won't do. Justice must be something we take seriously here and now. Once again the porridge has suddenly switched from hot to cold.

So far I have suggested a) that it is not so obvious that equality is the value that uniquely distinguishes socialists from their opponents; and b) that if we take material equality as the kind of equality which *might* play this distinguishing role, we find that its advocates tend to retreat when challenged to a position that is barely egalitarian at all (and hence, as in the case of Rawls' difference principle, plainly not distinctively socialist). I now want to give two more direct reasons for abandoning material equality as the guiding ideal of socialism, one practical, the other principled. For simplicity's sake I shall take *equality of incomes* as the ideal that is up for discussion, the qualifications to this that egalitarians like Cohen would wish to make not being germane to the present argument.

The practical objection is simply that income inequalities in market economies cannot be reduced beyond a certain point, and that in most countries the present trend appears to be moving slowly in the direction of greater inequality.[10] It is very tempting to blame the latter on the policies of right-wing governments, and these have certainly contributed, but there are also underlying factors which have to do with the technical requirements of employment, the changing pattern of working life and so forth. The increasing dispersal of incomes is partly a matter of the widening gap between highly qualified professionals and managers at one end and unskilled workers at the other, but also partly a matter of greater dispersion within skill groups, as a result of more part-time work, more freelance work, *et cetera*. Now it is possible to combat this trend to some degree, by one or both of two routes. The older route is progressive taxation plus redistribution in favour of low income groups. The arguments here have been well rehearsed, and I think it would now be generally agreed that there are definite limits to the equalising potential of this classic social-democratic approach. The newer route, rightly favoured in my view in the Commission's Report, involves getting people into the market from a more equal starting point, by increasing the skills level of the less skilled, by making it easier to acquire working capital, and so forth. This is an excellent approach, but it will probably work more effectively as an anti-poverty device, preventing people from dropping out of the bottom of the labour market, than as a device for reducing inequality between top and bottom. One reason is that as you approach the top, relative ability counts for progressively more. If you make singing lessons freely available, everyone's voice may improve, but since not everyone can be Pavarotti or k.d. lang, there may not be much effect on the earnings of these favoured few.[11]

I do not mean to imply that we should give up on any attempt to make (primary or secondary) incomes more equal. But I think we should be realistic about the obstacles to doing so, and also clearer – this is the main burden of my paper – about why income inequality concerns us. It is not because equality of incomes is a requirement of justice. The reason for this is simply – here I side with Bernard Williams, the main philosophical inspiration behind the Commission's report, against Cohen – that some income inequalities are *deserved*.

If one puts the point in a sufficiently abstract way, it might seem that there is no dispute about this. Both sides of the argument might agree on something like the following: income inequalities are just only when people are responsible for the behaviour that produces them. Thus if John and Bill have the same job opportunities, but John decides to work a full week while Bill decides to work half time and spend the rest of the week cultivating his rose garden, everyone agrees that it is fair that their incomes should be unequal. The disagreement arises because one side wants to expand the notion of responsibility in such a way that people can be held responsible for the effects of deploying their native talents, while the other wants to contract it so that only clear-cut choices, like Bill's, will count as grounds for having a less-than-equal income.

Let us call the second view the voluntary control interpretation of desert. It says that people can only deserve rewards and other benefits on the basis of features of their conduct which are directly under their control, such as their choices and efforts. In particular natural talents are excluded as a basis for desert: you cannot deserve greater income if your achievements depend on native intelligence or other endowments which are not themselves the product of voluntary effort or choice. One problem with this second view is to say what is going to count as a genuine choice. Make Bill into Belinda, make the choice into one between full-time work and part-time work plus childcare, and the problem comes more clearly into view.

A second problem, which I shall focus upon here, is that any achievement for which we might want to hold someone responsible is going to have background conditions for which they are *not* responsible. John may choose to work at a certain job, but he cannot take credit for the fact that he is living in a society which has the technical resources to make a job of that kind available – say a society in which it is *possible* to work as a computer programmer. So at the very least, the responsibility condition must be rewritten, following a suggestion of George Sher's, to say that people cannot deserve benefits on the basis of features for which they are not responsible and which are not possessed equally by everyone.[12] The point about natural talents is not just that they are contingencies for which their possessor is not responsible, but that they are distributed unequally between different people.

But now let us press a little harder on the idea that people only deserve in the morally relevant sense on the basis of those aspects of their performance that are under their voluntary control, such as effort. Consider a performance which depends on natural talent such as climbing Everest or playing a Beethoven concerto at concert level. In cases like this the performer must a) have chosen and worked to turn a natural ability like manual dexterity into a developed talent like musical skill; b) have decided to deploy the talent so as to produce the performance – to spend his evening playing a concerto rather than watching television at home. These choices and exertions are presumably what someone who adheres to the voluntary control idea would want to count as *genuine* desert bases. But now observe that these voluntary acts take place against the background of unchosen factors: on the one hand the performer's native talents, on the other his tastes and preferences (insofar as these are not themselves subject to choice). The person who decides that she wants to become a mountaineer does so on the basis of what she knows about her physical capacities, and also on the basis of her liking for being out in the open air. Of course tastes and preferences can to some extent be cultivated; but they are usually cultivated on the basis of other existing tastes and capacities.[13] My point is that a greater or lesser element of contingency enters even into those elements of performance that the narrow interpretation of desert would want to allow in as possible bases. If we say that the concert pianist deserves applause, not for his performance as such, since this depends in part on his natural talents, but for what is left over when the effect of natural talent is removed – the choice and effort involved in raising himself to this level – then we immediately have to recognise that his making those choices and efforts itself depends on contingencies which are not under his control. He did not choose to be born dextrous and with a good musical ear. Other people have not been confronted with the same range of options as this person.

We therefore stand at a parting of the ways. If we try to take seriously the idea that people can only deserve things when they are fully responsible for what they achieve – in the sense that the outcome was not affected by contingencies which impinge unequally on different people – we find that the scope of desert shrinks to vanishing point. We can never say, in a real case, that someone deserves rewards or benefits for what they have done, because it is always reasonable to assume that their performance was affected by factors for which they were not responsible. If on the other hand we want to retain the idea of desert, then we need to replace the strong responsibility condition I have been considering so far by something along the following lines: people are responsible for a performance when they intended the performance to have the outcome that it did, and when the performance depends in the right kind of way on qualities and characteristics that are integral to the performer, including her tastes and natural abilities. This excludes cases in which people bring about results inadvertently, or as some kind of fluke, or in which the outcome of their actions depends upon external conditions that affect different people differently, but leaves in as suitable bases for desert instances like the concert performance which combine effort and choice with natural talent and preference.

The upshot of this argument is that there is no half-way house between desert and radical egalitarianism. If you accept that inequalities are just when people deserve to enjoy different levels of benefit, then this must include cases where desert depends on natural talents. If, on the other hand, you want to exclude the effects of natural talents by saying that people only deserve different treatment when they are fully responsible for what they achieve, then you must end up by recommending strict equality. There will always be some external differentiating factor to account for the different efforts and choices that people make. I have not attempted to show that this second view is inherently untenable, but few people will, I believe, be happy with a view that turns its back so completely on notions of responsibility and free agency.

This concludes my case against taking material equality as the kind of equality that the Left should pursue. I have argued that there are serious practical limits to the pursuit of equality of this kind in market economies, and also that inequalities may be justified in principle by differences in peoples' deserts. But I do not want to conclude that we must simply fall back on equality of opportunity as our goal, even in the strong form favoured by Gordon Brown and the Commission. So let me now make the case for social equality as a distinctive principle of the Left, an ideal that neither Conservatives nor Liberals have shown any inclination to support.[14]

Let me try to elucidate further what I mean by social equality or *equality of status*. Equality of status obtains in a society when each member regards him- or herself as fundamentally the equal of all the others, and is regarded by the others as fundamentally their equal. It involves, then, the reciprocal recognition of equal standing. This does not mean that members regard one other as having equal standing in every sphere of activity in which they may engage: some will be regarded as better footballers than others, some as better architects, and so on and so forth. But these specific judgements will not crystallise into an overall social ranking such that we can assign people places in a hierarchy of social standing. The contrast here is with a ranked society in which there is consensus about where people stand in a more or less sharply defined system of social classes. People think of themselves as belonging to one or other of these classes, and interact with other individuals on the basis of norms and expectations governing inter- and intra-class relations. Typically there will be titles, special forms of address, conventional modes of displaying deference and so forth. Social ranking is clearly a matter of degree, and a society of equal status stands at the end of a spectrum the other end of which is occupied by a caste system in which inequalities of rank are fixed, pervasive and publicly affirmed.[15]

The appeal of an egalitarian society, the reason why social equality is widely valued, is that it aspires to be a society in which people deal with one another simply as individuals, taking account only of personal capacities, needs, achievements, etc without the blocking effect of status differences. I do not claim that this is a universally valued ideal. We can understand, if not sympathise with, aristocratic disdain for the easy familiarity between people implied by it. Nevertheless it seems to be an ideal that is widely endorsed in societies which are open and socially mobile, but still marked by class differences. The values at stake here can perhaps best be suggested by the responses invoked in a survey sample by the question "What sort of changes in social class in America would you like to see in the future, and why those?" Among those who favoured moving towards a classless society, the following reactions were typical:

Social class as a way of treating others should be eradicated. People should be treated equally.

I think everyone should be judged as a person, not by his job or how much money he has. Judging that way is the main thing wrong now.

I hope the time will come when everyone will get along as one class without regard for race, creed, and colour, and all these extraneous things like income and material well-being.[16]

Each of these reactions appears to pick up a different aspect of the ideal of an egalitarian society in which people's behaviour towards one another is not conditioned by differences of rank, in which specific inequalities – in income, say – do not crystallise into judgements of overall personal worth, and in which barriers of class do not stand in the way of mutual understanding and sympathy.

Social equality is not a principle of distributive justice. It does not tell us anything directly about how social institutions should assign benefits and burdens to individuals. It describes the overall character of a society, and it directs our attention to the way in which the members understand their relationship to one another. It does have *implications* for distributive justice, but only because the way in which we distribute goods and resources almost inevitably effects the way in which we regard one another. Certain kinds of material inequality may destroy social equality – but that is something that has to be established empirically, not demonstrated as a matter of conceptual necessity.

So what practical implications do follow from the ideal of social equality I have sketched? How can it guide our political thinking? I want to suggest three directions of advance.

The first is equal citizenship in a fairly strong sense. This corresponds to the first principle in the Commission's Report, but the idea would benefit from being spelt out more explicitly. It means first of all that every citizen should enjoy a set of rights that go beyond civil and political rights to embrace the social rights that make citizenship a real possibility: nobody can be an equal citizen while sleeping in a cardboard box on the Thames embankment. But citizenship should also be an active status, in that people should have the experience of interacting with one another on an equal footing in public settings. In particular they should be involved in the making of political decisions: it is of course not easy to translate this ideal into practice in a large and complex society, but I am convinced that citizenship cannot serve as a foundation for social equality unless it goes beyond the equal enjoyment of rights to become an active role. Finally here, it is important that there should be public spaces in which people congregate without distinction. It is one of the more alarming tendencies (from the point of view of the social egalitarian) in present-day society that schools, hospitals, even shopping precincts, are in danger of becoming socially segregated, so that people no longer rub shoulders with one another in places that emphasise their commonality (everyone gets ill, everyone needs education, and so forth). In thinking about these questions, we tend to focus on the injustice that is perpetrated by private medicine or private education, but we should not forget that social equality is also put at stake when people are able to cocoon themselves in private hospitals or schools.

The second direction in which social equality should point us is towards what Michael Walzer has called "complex equality".[17] This concerns the extent to which various types of social goods all accrue to the same people, or on the other hand are distributed in different, non-cumulative ways. Walzer attaches the label "complex equality" to a society in which many different goods – income, power, education, recognition, *et cetera* – are allocated by their own criteria of distribution in such a way that having more of good X gives a person no particular advantage in the competition for good Y. Assuming that the same person does not win out in all the spheres of distribution, such pluralism is likely to contribute to equality of status: if A outranks B in some spheres but B outranks A in others, this will make it difficult if not impossible to arrive at a consolidated ranking that would allow A and B to be assigned to separate classes.[18]

What follows from this practically is that we should try to preserve the independence of the various spheres, attempting as far as possible to prevent people from converting the advantages they gain in one sphere – money, say – into advantages in another – education or political power. We should also stop spheres from simply collapsing into one another, as would happen, for instance, if health care were to become simply another commodity whose distribution depended on each person's purchasing power. More positively, governments can act to expand spheres which can counteract those that threaten to become pre-eminent. In societies like our own, the most likely threat to complex equality comes from the sphere of money, which may dominate the other spheres in terms of people's perceptions of social status. This can be offset to some extent by fostering rival spheres. Consider the system of public honours. Under complex equality there will be various forms of public recognition of achievements that stand alongside, and can serve to offset, achievements in spheres such as those of money and power. Honours are distributed to people who have performed acts of public service, to artists and scientists, and to others whose contribution would perhaps not otherwise be given tangible recognition. This distribution can be more or less extensive, it can be done in a low-key or high-key way, and so forth. The underlying distributive principle is not up for negotiation, but its institutional expression is (within limits). So in a society in which money threatens to become a pre-eminent good, complex equality can be fortified by boosting the sphere of recognition, especially by making sure that the avenues of recognition are open to those who do not stand high in the other spheres. (If honours are given for charitable activity, they should go to those who are active in community service, say, not to those who are simply willing to write large cheques.) In a similar way, as Walzer himself has pointed out,[19] the extent of the spheres of education and welfare reflects political choices. The distributive criteria for these goods are determined internally to each sphere, but the size and shape of the budget, which establishes how much of the good there is to distribute in the first place, is decided by the state.

If a strong form of equal citizenship could be established, and inequalities in the distribution of specific goods were allowed to offset one another in the manner envisaged by Walzer, would social egalitarians need to worry any further about economic inequality? Would big income differences matter against the background of equal citizenship and compensating inequalities in other goods? I think that they still would. Where income differences are very large, this will almost inevitably create a segregated society in which people live very different styles of life and associate socially almost entirely with those on similar incomes. The complex equality approach to social equality is hard to sustain in the face of an income distribution such as the one that now exists in Britain. So we have to tackle the issue of income distribution, but on the basis of reducing differentials to a size that is not destructive of social equality rather than on the basis of attempting to reduce them to zero.

At this point my argument rests on a kind of wager whose character I should spell out explicitly. The wager is this: if we can establish what scale of economic inequalities people deserve, by virtue of their efforts, skills, talents, the responsibilities they bear and so forth, the magnitudes in question are not so great as to be destructive of social equality. It would be silly to try to put precise figures on this, but purely as a thought experiment, imagine a society in which economic enterprises paid their members incomes whose top-to-bottom differential was no greater than four to one. If pay were profit related, this might mean a differential of twice that amount between the top manager of a successful company and an unskilled worker in a less successful one. Could a society whose top income was £80,000 and whose bottom income was £10,000 be socially egalitarian in the sense I have been elucidating? I think that it could, in circumstances of equal citizenship and Walzerian complex equality, bearing in mind that the differential between the two token individuals will not in practice be a rigid one, but will vary over the course of their lives and according to the relative fortunes of their enterprises. Now if we ask people to say what they regard as fair income differentials for people doing jobs of various kinds, they will volunteer figures very much of that order. So the wager may turn out to be a reasonable one. Rather than having to choose between desert and equality, as it is often suggested we must, we could aim for a society in which people's different deserts were properly recognised, but there was still overall social equality, or what I have been calling equality of status.

But how to get the differentials down to roughly the size suggested in the previous paragraph? The Report's proposals go some way in the right direction, but I believe that we have eventually to bite the bullet and say that we won't get a socially just or an equal society without tackling the system of ownership and control that characterises the modern capitalist firm or corporation. The offensively inflated salaries paid to top executives of which we have recently had a large spate are more or less the inevitable result of the concentration of decision-making power in boards of directors who are nominally responsible to their shareholders but not to their employees. Some form of market socialism is, I believe, the only way to reduce differentials to the size that people generally believe to be fair.[20] Since market socialism, once thought to be a rather timid idea, is now regarded by many on the Left as dangerously radical, equality too remains a radical idea. But at least the equality that I've tried to defend is somewhere on the map of political possibilities, whereas the equality I've been criticising – material equality, equality of resources – is so far off it as to be utopian in the derogatory sense.

Endnotes

1. In writing this paper I have drawn freely on three longer pieces of work: "Equality and Market Socialism "in P K Bardhan and J Roemer (eds.) (1993) *Market Socialism: the Current Debate*, New York: Oxford University Press; "Complex Equality "in D Miller and M Walzer (eds.) (1995) *Pluralism, Justice and Equality*, Oxford: Clarendon Press; "Two Cheers for Meritocracy", *Journal of Political Philosophy* (forthcoming).

2. R Hattersley "Balance of Power", *The Guardian*, July 25 1996, p. 15; G Brown, "In the Real World", *The Guardian*, August 2 1996, p. 13.

3. *The Justice Gap*, London: IPPR (1993), p. 16; and *Social Justice: Strategies for National Renewal*, London: Vintage (1994), p. 18.

4. GA Cohen "Back to Socialist Basics", *New Left Review*, 207 (Sept/Oct 1994), p. 6.

5. *ibid*, p. 11.

6. Eg W Letwin (ed) (1983) *Against Equality*, London: Macmillan.

7. W Kymlicka (1990) *Contemporary Political Philosophy*, Oxford: Clarendon Press.

8. R Dworkin (1989) "Equality of Resources", *Philosophy and Public Affairs*, 10, 283-345. For Dworkin's opposition to socialism see R Dworkin, (1991) "Confronting the end of the socialist era", *Economy and Society*, 20, 341-9, and my reply "The relevance of socialism "in the same issue, pp. 350-62.

9. J Rawls (1971) *A Theory of Justice*, Cambridge, Mass.: Harvard University Press, ch. 2.

10. I rely here on A B Atkinson "Income Distribution in Europe and the United States", Discussion Paper no. 103, Nuffield College, Oxford (Sept. 1995).

11. This argument has been spelt out at greater length in M. Kaus (1992) *The End of Equality*, New York: Basic Books, as part of a more general argument for "Civic Liberalism" as against "Money Liberalism". Although some of the problems and solutions canvassed in the book are distinctively American, I believe it deserves to be more widely discussed outside the US. The kind of equality that Kaus wants to defend is similar to that defended in the present paper. Kaus goes on to argue, however, that reducing inequalities in income and wealth is essentially irrelevant to the pursuit of social equality, and here I part company with him, for reasons to be given later.

12. See G Sher (1987) *Desert*, Princeton: Princeton University Press, ch. 2.

13. On this point see AT "Talent Pooling" in J R Pennock and J W Chapman (eds.) (1981) *Nomos 23: Human Rights*, New York: New York University Press.

14. It is true that John Major has occasionally expressed his support for "the classless society" but this turns out on closer inspection to mean simply a meritocracy, *ie* a society in which your social position depends on your achievements and not your inherited status.

15. As Kaus reminds us, one of the best evocations of what a society that had achieved social equality might look like can be found in Orwell's description of revolutionary Barcelona in *Homage to Catalonia*.

16. Quoted in R P Coleman and L Rainwater (1979) *Social Standing in America*, London: Routledge and Kegan Paul, pp. 299-300.

17. M Walzer (1983) *Spheres of Justice*, Oxford: Martin Robertson.

18. For a much fuller defence of Walzer's argument here, see my paper "Complex equality".

19. M Walzer (1993) "Exclusion, Injustice, and the Democratic State", *Dissent*, 40, pp. 63-4.

20. For discussion of market socialism, see J Le Grand and S Estrin (eds) (1989) *Market Socialism*, Oxford: Clarendon Press, and my own more elaborate defence in *Market, State, and Community: theoretical foundations of market socialism*, Oxford: Clarendon Press, (1989).

What has Socialism to do with Sexual Equality?[1]

Anne Phillips

What has socialism to do with sexual equality? At the most general level, that equality is central to socialism, and that equality includes equality between women and men. But the meaning of equality has been widely contested, and this level of generality does not take us very far. Karl Marx was always rather sniffy about empty claims to equality, and his preferred objective – "from each according to his ability, to each according to his needs" - seems entirely compatible with a division of labour that allocates different responsibilities to women and men. Later socialists have been more willing make equality a core value, but they have disagreed over the appropriate balance between equality of opportunity and equality of outcomes, and they have varied widely in their understanding of what it is that has to be equalised. The idea that domestic work, for example, should be distributed equally between women and men, was a relatively late development even in feminist circles: as Ellen DuBois has noted in her discussion of nineteenth century suffragists, "'sharing housework' may be a more uniquely twentieth-century feminist demand than 'smashing monogamy'".[2]

Equalising either housework or childcare certainly did not figure large in nineteenth century socialist debate. The so-called utopian socialists tended to favour co-operative arrangements for domestic work or bringing up children. But this derived from their critique of the privatised (self-interested) family, rather than any preoccupation with redistributing work between women and men.[3] Later in the century, Marxists tended to regard women's confinement to the domestic sphere as the key factor in their subordination to men, and looked to the fuller participation of women in socialised production as the means to their emancipation. In Engels' over-optimistic extrapolation from the employment of women in the textile industry, this process was already well under way; in August Bebel's *Women and Socialism,*[4] the emancipation through work had to be combined with a programme for socialising domestic labour. Instead of each woman being condemned to her own private oven and sink, there would be central kitchens and public laundries, centralised heating arrangements and centralised cleaning services. That the cooks and the cleaners might continue to be women was not, at this stage, considered an issue.

The alternative argument from the nineteenth century was that a genuinely unconfined free market should be enough to deliver sexual equality. This, largely, is what John Stuart Mill argued in his essay on *The Subjection of Women*,[5] where he identified the subjection of women as the main surviving remnant of an earlier social order, and increasingly at odds with the defining principle of modern society. He took this to be the notion that competition and not birth should be what dictates a person's position in life: that instead of our life-chances being determined by the accidents of birth, what we do or become should be a matter that is decided by free competition. "Nobody", as Mill put it, "thinks it necessary to make a law that only a strong-armed man shall be a blacksmith. Freedom and competition suffice to make blacksmiths strong armed men, because the weak-armed can earn more by engaging in occupations for which they are more fit."[6] What, then, was added by the plethora of nineteenth century legislation that prohibited women from even entering the competitive arena? If the principle of freedom and competition is true, he argued, "we ought to act as if we believed it, and not to ordain that to be born a girl instead of a boy, any more than to be born black instead of white, or a commoner instead of a nobleman, shall decide the person's position through all life – shall interdict people from all the more elevated social positions, and from all, except a few, respectable occupations."[7]

As is apparent from some of his other writings, Mill was not an unambiguous supporter of free competition. He was also very much taken with the case for co-operative ownership, and he sympathised with many of the socialist arguments of his contemporaries. As far as sexual equality was concerned, however, he did seem to think an unconfined free market – unconfined, that is, by legislation that dictated differential treatment for women and men – should be enough to deliver the desired result. Mill neither anticipated nor desired a world in which men and women would take on the same range of work or responsibilities; he did not expect men to take an equal share of domestic work or childcare; and in common with many economists of his time (and later), he believed that too great an influx of women into the labour market would drag down wage levels and make everyone substantially worse off. What mattered was that women should be educated and enabled to support themselves, freed from the legal prohibitions that limited their educational and job opportunities, and released from the inequities in marriage law that made marriage a relationship between master and slave. But once marriage and motherhood had been transformed into a genuinely free choice and consensual arrangement, most women would surely opt gladly for their conventional role.

If we take these as exemplars of the more sexually egalitarian wings of the socialist and liberal traditions, it is evident that both traditions can generate a commitment to sexual equality. Whatever the historical errors or theoretical failings in Engels' *Origin of the Family, Private Property and the State*,[8] no one reading his analysis of male domination and female subjugation can doubt the importance he attached to achieving equality between women and men. And while the popularity of Bebel's *Women and Socialism* owed more to its much-needed vision of the future socialist society than its specific arguments on women, the book did go through more than 50 editions by the time of his death in 1913 to become one of the most widely read texts in the German socialist movement. Mill's writings on sexual equality attracted less contemporary attention that his other works on political theory or political economy, but his consistent backing for most of the central campaigns of nineteenth century feminism helped secure a close relationship between liberalism and first wave feminism. Neither the socialist nor the liberal tradition has proved itself a strong or consistent supporter of sexual equality; but both can make some claim to being its "natural home".

If there is any basis, from this earlier period, for claiming a special affinity with socialism, it lies in the socialist critique of privacy, and the way this alerted socialists to the peculiar constraints of the domestic sphere. Liberals were far more likely to defend private spaces against public regulation, and much less likely to regard the household as a place of confinement. Even allowing for Mill's strong condemnation of marital slavery, this made them more inclined to accept some version of "separate spheres". Socialists, by contrast, tended to distrust privacy as inherently individualistic and limiting, and in their celebration of collective activity and socialised production, they were considerably more disparaging of domestic life. For many, this simply spilled over into a disdain for women. For the minority, however, who bothered to address the so-called "Woman Question", it generated more consistent support for women's entry into the labour market than yet figured in the liberal tradition, as well as more imaginative proposals for transforming the conditions under which domestic work was carried out. The difference between the two traditions has sometimes been theorised as a difference between pursuing equality of opportunities and achieving equality of outcomes: liberalism typically focusing on removing the *legal* constraints to free up equality of opportunities; socialism typically addressing the *structural* conditions that are necessary to substantial equality.[9] But in its origins, at least, the difference stems as much from the liberal defence of private spaces and the socialist critique of private confinement.

Though the latter offered a basis for allying feminism to the socialist tradition, most of those active in the earlier feminist campaigns found a more congenial home within the liberal camp. Legal constraints and prohibitions were a particularly pressing concern through the late nineteenth century and early twentieth centuries; and while few liberals showed any great enthusiasm for women's emancipation, those who did gave active support to feminist campaigns. Socialists, meanwhile, tended to play the class card to trump any excessive preoccupation with sexual equality. When Selina Cooper, for example, argued the case for women's suffrage at the 1905 Labour Party Conference, Harry Quelch of the (Marxist) Social Democratic Federation announced that "Mrs Cooper has placed sex first ... we have to put Labour first in every case."[10] In the hierarchy of socialist concerns, sexual equality usually came low down the list.

A rather different pattern emerged in the early years of the contemporary women's movement, when feminists found themselves more closely attuned to the socialist than the liberal tradition. Debates through the 1970s were often ordered through a three-way split between liberal, socialist and radical feminists and, in Britain, the overwhelming majority placed themselves in the second or third camp. Previous campaigns had removed many of the more overt legal inequalities, thereby reducing some of the attractions of liberal feminism. But the connections that were made with socialism were also specific to the historical moment, for they reflected a wider political context in which socialism had come to set the terms for radical social critique. Many of the early activists came from a prior involvement in left politics, and even in distancing themselves from socialism, feminists often reproduced its analytical traditions. For example, one of the key texts in the development of a radical (ie non-socialist) feminism was Shulamith Firestone's *Dialectic of Sex*,[11] but Firestone employed a Marxist terminology to identify women as a distinct "sex-class". Several years later, radical feminists in Britain described themselves, somewhat confusingly, as "revolutionary feminists". In the formative years of the women's liberation movement, the socialist tradition still had a monopoly on the language of radicalism. The later discovery that the right could also be radical came as rather a shock.

Where there was a more substantial theoretical basis to the partnership of socialism with feminism, it lay in the socialist equation of domesticity with confinement, and the socialist preference for whatever was collective, public, and social. Few feminists went along with the idea that women's emancipation would occur simply through their entry into socialised production. But the notion that sexual inequality was rooted in women's confinement to the private household fitted well with the preoccupations of the 1950s and 1960s: the critique of housework, for example, as a thankless and repetitive cycle in which nothing new was ever created; or the critique of the nuclear family, as requiring women to sacrifice their integrity and personality to the nurture of husbands who would come to despise them, and children whose first task on reaching maturity would be to push their mothers aside. Feminists in the 1990s are far more likely to dwell on the double burden women experience in juggling the demands of paid employment with the care responsibilities that continue to fall almost exclusively on their shoulders. In the formative literature, by contrast, attention was more typically focused on the way that women were silenced, marginalised, turned in on themselves, encouraged to look to fulfilment through finding the "right man", discouraged from any more public activity. In principle, at least, the liberal language of individuality and freedom offered an equally powerful resource for addressing these issues. But liberalism was regarded as condoning a sharp separation between public and private spheres, and turning a blind eye to what went on in the household. This hardly tuned in with the aspirations of those who were experimenting with alternative forms of collective living and collective childcare, nor did it have much to say to those who were developing an analysis of male violence. (Not that this last was a strong point among socialists either.)

The distance travelled since then is enormous. For feminists, the most important milestones have been the failure to establish sustainable alternatives to the nuclear family; the steady increase in women's paid employment, which has made the double burden so much more central to feminist analysis; and the disenchantment with that combination of full time employment for women, under-staffed and over-regulated nurseries for children, which characterised so many of the state socialist societies. In her periodisation of feminist approaches to motherhood (based on American experience, but comparable to what happened in Britain) Ann Snitow[12] notes the self-questioning of motherhood that characterised so many of the key texts of the 1970s: the attempt to detach being a woman from the requirement to be a mother; but also the attempt to detach biological motherhood from the responsibilities of caring for children. This contrasts markedly with a subsequent celebration of motherhood as generating distinct values of nurture and care.

In this later phase, the quintessentially feminist programme has been a reorganisation of paid employment (more substantial parental leave, more part-time work for both women and men, more flexibility in employment patterns) so that both mothers *and* fathers can divide their time equitably between parenthood and work. The idea that parenting could be socialised, either through better social provision of child care services, or through collective living arrangements that draw both parents and non-parents into responsibilities for caring for children, has given way to a more privatised scenario, in which individual mothers and fathers will be enabled to reach a more egalitarian division of their domestic labour. Not that social provision has dropped out of the programme: improving and expanding nursery provision, for example, remains a central feminist concern. But feminists are less inclined to view care work just as a "burden" to be lifted from their shoulders onto those of the state. They are also less prepared to view sexual equality as something that changes women's lives without more substantially changing the men's.

Over the same period, socialists have also made their peace with privacy. It is no longer presumed that social ownership must be better than private; it is no longer presumed that collective arrangements must be better than individual ones; it is no longer presumed that people find their fulfilment in socialised production, or are lessened by watching a video in the privacy of their home. Though the current flurry around community or communitarianism testifies to continuing anxieties about the scale of this shift, most socialists have backed away from the critique of privacy that was so characteristic of the earlier tradition. Most, indeed, have refashioned their socialism to give more place to the individual, and the rights and freedoms of this individual (which may include the right to opt out of trade unions or out of socialised provision in education or health) are now regarded as eminently suitable socialist concerns.

Where does this leave any special affinity between socialism and sexual equality? Oddly, it seems, much stronger. Today's socialists are more consistently attuned to the requirements of sexual equality than their predecessors; and in Britain, as elsewhere in Europe, it has been parties on the left of the political spectrum that have been most willing to adopt measures of positive action to speed up the process of change.[13] The Labour party is certainly more tuned in than it has been to the issues and problems that confront women, as evidenced in its commitment to recruiting more women as political representatives, and in the impressively "feminised" understanding of the contemporary labour market that underpins the Report of the Commission on Social Justice. But this growing affinity with sexual equality may owe more to the recent convergence between liberal and socialist values (and the associated downgrading of class) than to anything specific to the socialist tradition. What does socialism have to add to the project of sexual equality? Can sexual equality can be achieved within a broadly liberal framework that recognises the equal worth of all individuals, regardless of their sex? Or is socialism – and if so, what kind of socialism – a necessary condition for sexual equality?

Equality in contemporary socialist thought

David Miller argues that the attachment to (some kind of) equality does not uniquely distinguish socialists from their opponents;[14] we might equally well note that the attachment to (some kind of) liberty does not uniquely distinguish liberals from their opponents. Today's socialists are very much preoccupied with the relationship between equality and freedom, and most would like to arrive at some trade-off between these two that weights them relatively evenly. One expression of this is the rather disparaging dismissal of strict equality (the "leveller's strategy") that we find in the Report of the Commission on Social Justice; another is the recovery of equality of opportunities as a far more radical strategy than its critics used to admit.

Thus the Commission on Social Justice argues for what Stuart White describes as an "endowment egalitarianism" that equalises the initial distribution of capabilities and skills, primarily through education and training.[15] It presents this as an attractive alternative to the more conventional redistribution of income. If the alternative worked, it would short-circuit the equalisation-after-the-event that characterises policies of progressive taxation. Instead of waiting for the inequalities to emerge – and then taxing the rich to pay for the poor – it should be possible to intervene at an earlier stage to equalise life-chances and job opportunities. What makes this particularly attractive in the present political climate is that it promises to ease the tension between equality and freedom. Instead of relying on an interventionist state to deliver more substantial equality of income, people will be equalised to make their own choices, and make what they can of their lives. Such a strategy is in many ways limited: it seems to accept the slots that are becoming available in an economy that divides jobs more starkly than before into full-time or part-time, high-paid or low-paid, relatively secure or inherently transient, but calls for a more radical understanding of social and job mobility that will empower individuals to move more freely and equally between these slots.[16] That said, the equal opportunities that are implied in the strategy are considerably more substantial that the equal right to enter the competitive arena. They carry with them a strong commitment to eliminating the early patterns of disadvantage that weave their way around children as they enter the educational system, and they anticipate extensive social intervention to equalise initial endowments. The Commission on Social Justice goes, indeed, considerably further even than this, for it construes equal opportunities as including a life-time chance to regain ground that was lost at an earlier stage. The idea is not just to equalise our starting positions, and then condone whatever inequalities subsequently emerge. The emphasis on "lifelong learning" suggests that some of the subsequent inequalities must also be tackled – particularly those that relate to inequalities in education and skills.

The other modification to socialist thinking, heavily influenced by developments in liberal and libertarian theory, is to say that inequalities are justified when they arise from individual choice or effort, but unjustified when they arise from "brute-luck". This produces a peculiar amalgam of what used to be viewed as distinctively socialist and liberal traditions, for while the distinction potentially challenges any inequalities arising from inherited wealth (the brute-luck of being born to rich parents), it also condones what may be very substantial inequalities of income, so long as these derive from individual effort or choice. The emphasis, again, is on resolving tensions between equality and freedom. The inequalities that have prevented individuals from making their equal choices should be eliminated; but the inequalities that arise from the exercise of this personal choice need not.

This is quite a startling modification of egalitarian ideals, but the standard examples offered in its defence are not particularly controversial. Most people will say it is fair enough for John to earn more than Bill if he has chosen to work longer hours; most people, indeed, will say it is fair enough that those who have chosen to sacrifice their early earning potential by staying on at school or university should later benefit from higher incomes. The problem, as David Miller has noted, is that it is hard to determine what counts as genuine choice, and he uses an example taken from the differences between women and men to illustrate some of the difficulties. We may all agree that John is entitled to more income than Bill if he has chosen to work more intensely and for longer hours, but do we really think John is entitled to more than Belinda, who chose part-time work in order to combine it with looking after her children? The woman who chooses to work part-time therefore "chooses" not only a lower income overall, but very often a job that offers lower hourly pay and minimal job protection; she makes this choice, however, against a background of structural constraints that include her responsibilities to what are still considered "her" children. Virtually all of our choices are structured in some way by the society in which we live, and there may not be much left that is unambiguously chosen. Why should people be required to live with the consequences of their "choice" when they had so little alternative? If inequalities are to be regarded as unjustified when they arise from circumstances beyond our control, does this not lead us back to notions of strict equality?

I shall return to this question later. For the moment, I just want to note that the renewed interest in equality of opportunities combines with the attempt to distinguish brute-luck from chosen inequalities to encourage a closer alliance between socialism and sexual equality. Establishing equal opportunities in education and employment has always figured as a major concern in the feminist project (and has often been downgraded by previous socialists because of its overtly individualistic basis). The renewed emphasis on equal opportunities then provides a strong link to issues of sexual equality. The brute-luck argument looks even more congenial, for any inequalities that can be attributed to the good luck of being born a boy or the bad luck of being born a girl fall self-evidently into the category of unjustified inequalities. (The argument is then reminiscent of Mill's argument in *The Subjection of Women*.) So while the recent shifts in socialist thinking have moderated the stricter egalitarianism of an earlier period, they have also been peculiarly favourable to the arguments for equality between women and men. Much of this, of course, reflects the accommodation socialists have now reached with key elements in the liberal tradition. This suggests that it is the marriage of socialism with liberalism that now offers the best hope for sexual equality.

Sexual equality as strict equality

So far, so cosy. What I want to argue, however, is that sexual equality is one area where we continue to need strong notions of *strict equality*. None of the economic inequalities between women and men is particularly hard to explain, for whether we look at the sexual distribution of full-time and part-time employment, or the disproportionate number of women in jobs that require minimal training, or the difficulties women experience in reaching the higher levels on any career ladder, they all point to the unequal division of care work that requires so many women to interrupt their working lives, or opt for part time employment. There is also, of course, overt discrimination, but we do not have to resort to any great conspiracy theory to explain the wage gap between the sexes. Underlying all the sexual inequalities in the labour market is the persistent association between women and care work, and I can see no way out of this short of equalising this work between women and men. This is an argument for strict equality.

As long as boys and girls continue to grow up with such different expectations of the way they will balance out work and family, this will inevitably affect the choices they make in developing their "endowments". As long as women continue to find themselves with the primary responsibility for caring for the young, the sick or the elderly, this will inevitably translate into systematic disadvantage on the labour market. If the post-war expansion of women's employment tells us anything, it is that the sexes cannot be equal in their job opportunities when they are so profoundly different in their domestic lives. Unless the responsibilities of care work are equalised between women and men (which depends not only on the level of social provision, but also on major restructuring of the hours and conditions of paid employment), women's income, position, and conditions will continue to reflect the bad luck of being born female.

The argument is most powerful as applied to sexual inequalities in the labour market, but it also extends to such matters as male violence against women. The association between masculinity and aggression – and the much higher incidence of male violence towards women than female violence towards men – can hardly be explained by the fact that men are, on average, bigger and stronger. If this were the explanation, we would be able to identify potential rapists simply by height and strength. The more probable explanation lies in the markedly different expectations our cultures lay on women and men, most of which relate to the sexual division of responsibilities for care. Requiring men to rock their babies to sleep or look after parents with Alzheimer's disease may not, of itself, reduce the incidence of rape. But it does not take great theoretical sophistication to perceive the connection between the sexual division of carework and the norms of masculine behaviour.

I am not claiming that a more equitable distribution of care work between women and men resolves all problems of sexual inequality, for while I do see the sexual division of labour as crucial in sustaining sexual hierarchies and oppressions, I would not want to present equality in employment and care work as the only feminist concern. Nor would I want to argue that a more equitable distribution between mothers and fathers resolves all problems of care work: I think there is a great deal still to be said about the closures of the nuclear family; and even if we set this to one side, a significant number of parents (overwhelmingly women) are bringing up children on their own, and depend crucially on social provision for child-care and other services. I am saying, however, that *any* inequality between women and men is unjustified. Whatever other conclusions we may reach about justified and unjustified inequalities of income, or justified and unjustified inequalities of power, there can be no justification for a distribution of income or power that is skewed by sex, any more than for one that is skewed by race.

Similar conclusions emerge if we switch from individual entitlement to consider the social distribution of incomes as a whole. In his discussion of comprehensive egalitarianism, David Miller shifts the basis of the argument away from what individuals might or might not be entitled to, and towards the degree of inequality that a society can accept as compatible with recognising equality of status. What we may deserve then becomes of secondary importance. Whether the poor are "deserving" or not, there is a limit to how much a society premised on equal status can condone people living in abject poverty; whether the rich are "deserving" or not, there is a limit to the range of income differential that is compatible with an egalitarian society. There is, in Miller's view, no requirement for strict equality, and he rules this out as incompatible with personal autonomy. Societies can and must live with a certain degree of income inequality, but it is impossible to regard all citizens as enjoying equal standing when the disparities become too grotesque.

As applied to specifically sexual inequalities, however, this argument seems to confirm the case for strict equality. It certainly implies that the income differentials between women and men should not be so large as to undermine any notion of equal standing between the sexes. But the notion of equal status would have to go considerably further, for any income differential that seemed to be tied to one's sex or race would surely be incompatible with equality of status. An egalitarian society might be able to live with a one to four income differential, but could it live with the notion that being born female, or being born black, had condemned one to the lower half of that scale? And if it could not live with this, would this not imply that the sexes must be distributed in roughly equal proportions across the full range of income inequalities?

Though this all seems terribly obvious to me, I am aware that it is not so obvious to everyone else. For most people, I think, the argument carries more conviction when it is applied to the distribution of ethnic groups than when it is applied to the distribution of women and men. If it can be established that one's chances in the labour market are related to the colour of one's skin, most people will see this as unjustified. (When people defend racial inequalities in employment, they tend to argue that what appears to be an effect of race is in reality an effect of class.) But if it can be established that one's chances in the labour market are related to one's sex, many people still view this with equanimity, for they see it as a "natural" enough consequence of women's role as mothers, and the way this affects their patterns of employment. It may be unfortunate, but is not necessarily seen as unfair. Indeed, it is far more likely to be seen as a matter of the choices that women have made. It is not only men who will say this, for women do see themselves as having a choice in the matter, and many (very sensibly) opt for the pleasures of motherhood over the intensities of contemporary employment. The issue then comes back to what counts as genuine choice. Do we say this was not a genuine choice because it was made within certain constraints? Or is that setting such a high standard for choice that it renders the term virtually meaningless?

If we say that nothing counts as a choice unless it was made from a full range of options, we are, I think, emptying the word of its meaning. All the choices we make are made within certain constraints, but that does not mean they were not choices. I cannot choose to be an opera singer because I do not have the necessary voice, but that does not stop me feeling I make genuine choices between the other options at my disposal. I cannot vote for my ideal party because that party does not exist, but that does not stop me feeling I make genuine choices between the parties that contest an election. Neither of these restrictions, however, marks me out from anyone else. We all lack the necessary talents for something we would have liked to pursue; we all have political aspirations that no party has yet promised to meet. The point about sexual or racial inequality is that the range of choices has been restricted in a blanket fashion by the characteristics of sex or race: the accident of being born female or black, into a society where this still structures our lives.

I owe this formulation to John Stuart Mill – to the exemplar of the liberal rather than the socialist tradition – but in my view it leads to a much stricter equality than was ever envisaged by Mill. The accident of being born male or female no longer carries significant consequences in the field of legal entitlement, and has rapidly decreasing consequences in the field of education. It still has very significant effects, however, on the responsibilities the individual assumes for care work, and on the positions the individual occupies in employment or politics. Sex remains a major predictor of an individual's life-chances, and wherever this is the case, there is a prima facie case for equalisation. It is not just a matter, as the Report of the Commission on Social Justice puts it, of men taking on "*some* (my emphasis) of the caring responsibilities previously carried by women".[17] Any inequality that arises from being female should simply be ruled out of court.

To rephrase this, we might say that there is no significant space between equality of opportunities and equality of outcomes when it comes to sexual or racial equality. If the outcomes turn out to be statistically related to sex or race, then the opportunities were clearly not equal. If we assume that talents and predilections are roughly equally distributed among the sexes, then the only explanation for a disproportionate concentration of men in certain kinds of activities and a disproportionate concentration of women in others must be the social structures and conventions that constrain our development. The very fact that men and women end up occupying different positions in the distribution of work and influence and income is evidence enough of unjustified inequality. What else, short of some genetic imbalance, could explain it? (I will not consider here the further questions that might arise if a future generation of psychologists managed to prove some genetic distinction, and whether that would then count as a justification for sexual inequality. I do not see that it would, but given the immense difficulties in separating out genetic from environmental factors, it is not a problem that is likely to face us.) Wherever there is a systematic differentiation between the sexes – in the distribution of jobs or care work or influence or incomes – this alerts us to unjustified inequality. The only inequalities we can possibly justify are those that relate to features other than sex or race.

Up to this point, I have reserved judgement on the wider issue. I have argued that, whatever distinction we may make between justified and unjustified inequalities, sexual and racial inequalities will always fall into the second camp. Let me now make some attempt at the wider issue. Should sex and race be regarded as

exceptional? And if so, why? I suggested earlier that it was the
blanket nature of sexual and racial inequalities that marked them
out from other chance restrictions on our opportunities or
outcomes: that we can accommodate inequalities that derive from
individual variations (being tone-deaf, being physically
uncoordinated, being good or bad at maths), but cannot
accommodate those that derive from blanket injunctions. Yet in
either case, we are dealing with the accidents of birth. All
inequalities of power or income must arise either from an inequality
in social conditions, or else from an unequal inheritance of
capacities and talents, among which we must surely include the
capacity for hard work.[18] From a socialist perspective, the first
looks self-evidently unjust. The second also seems unfair, for these
things are hardly under our control. The problem with the second,
however, is that we cannot just legislate all these differences away,
for if we did, we would end up eliminating much of what we value
in life.

It is not really fair, for example, that those with a gift for
language should be better placed to influence decisions than those
who find it hard to articulate their opinions, and it is particularly
unfair when the class bias in educational opportunities skews this
in favour of certain social groups. But even if we managed to
eliminate the class bias, there would still be differences of
personality and ability that made some individuals more persuasive
than others. The only way to eliminate this would be to end all
political discussion, and we would hardly be happy with this.[19] It
may also seem unfair, to follow a line of argument much loved by
Robert Nozick,[20] that an individual born with a Grecian profile
should have a better sex life than an individual born with a snub
nose. But if the only way to deal with this is to allocate sexual
partners at random, thereby eliminating any element of personal
choice, we would hardly be happy with this. We cannot legislate
against all accidents of birth, and to this extent, we are stuck with
some inevitable level of inequality. What we need is some way of
distinguishing the inevitable *individual* variations (some people are
just more lucky than others) from those associated with more
blanket injunctions. From a socialist perspective, this second
category would certainly include the disabilities that flow from

one's class; it should also include the disabilities that flow from one's sex or the colour of one's skin.

I do not pretend that this is an easy distinction, for all differences between individuals lend themselves to a group classification (the class of people who are tone-deaf, for example, and by virtue of this group characteristic, are denied the chance to work in the music business), and what one person defines as bad luck will be perceived by another as a blanket injunction. I also recognise that arguments for strict equality can be modified by pragmatic concerns. I would argue, for example, that inherited inequalities of wealth are always unjustified, but given the widespread desire to pass on to one's children the benefits built up through one's life, it may be impossible to get majority support for 100 per cent tax on inheritance. In similar vein, I would argue that sexual inequalities in power or income are always unjustified, but I would accept a strategy that started with some initial redistribution and worked up towards equal shares; or that started with increasing the proportion of women in male-dominated occupations, and built up towards full gender parity. In this, as in any area of social policy, one cannot hope to do everything overnight. The final aim, however, must surely be to eliminate inequalities associated with sex. I can see no normative basis for stopping short of full sexual equality.

Socialism as a condition for sexual equality

It is at this point that the special affinity between socialism and sexual equality comes more sharply to the fore. Sexual equality, as I understand it, depends on a major restructuring of the relationship between paid and unpaid labour so as to detach this division from the distinction between women and men. Sexual equality cannot be achieved simply through socialised provision of services (more nurseries, more home helps and meals on wheels, more homes for the disabled or the mentally ill or the elderly), for while these can certainly help equalise conditions for women and men, they do so by shifting care responsibilities from women working in the privacy of their home to (usually) women employed by the state. There are necessary limits to this strategy, for none of us wants a world in

which care work is entirely institutionalised. The strategy also
leaves untouched the differential roles of women and men. It will
still be women who do the work; it will still be women who depend
on the services. When these are threatened or removed, it will still
be women who have to carry the consequences. The longer term
solution lies combining socialised care provision with a new
balance between paid and unpaid work. This ultimately depends
on restructuring the hours and patterns of employment, for men as
well as for women.

The kinds of policies necessary to achieve this range from what
is already practised in some social democracies (notably in
Scandinavia) to what we can hardly begin to imagine. They would
include substantial periods of paid parental leave that could be
taken by either mothers or fathers; a requirement on employers to
offer reduced working hours to any employees (male or female)
who carry major responsibilities for caring for the young, sick or
old; additional rights to periods of unpaid leave that would allow
people to break their employment without losing their right to their
job; and, most important of all, a major reduction in the hours,
and alteration in the shifts, of *male* employment, so that male
workers are equally enabled to assume their caring responsibilities.
To put this more generally, the necessary changes would involve a
final, much belated, recognition that the typical worker is no longer
a man with a housewife in tow, and a reordering of the priorities
of employment to recognise that all of us have a great deal to do
outside the factory and office.

Left to its own devices, an unregulated market economy can
never deliver this. The market is no great respecter of sexual
distinction when it comes to employment practices: there has been
no wringing of hands over the decline of male employment in the
old bases of manufacturing industry and the simultaneous increase
in female employment; the market has not stepped in to restore
masculine pride. But while we may well rely on the forces of free
competition to equalise participation rates between women and
men, we cannot rely on these forces to reshape the hours and
conditions of work. It is, indeed, one of the appalling ironies of
the present period that high levels of unemployment coincide with
an extraordinary intensification of work for those lucky enough to

find jobs, and that the very insecurities of the job market have exposed people to longer and more unsocial hours. The market will happily release a significant proportion of adults from the constraints of paid employment, but it does this only to doom others to workaholic excess, and we cannot realistically rely on this market to establish sensible divisions between paid employment, care work, and leisure. Only a direct political initiative, underpinned by a strong commitment to sexual equality, could put the necessary changes in place.

Having said that, the kind of socialism required to achieve this may not be particularly radical. When Karl Marx examined the struggles in nineteenth century Britain to reduce the length of the working day, he argued that when the restrictions were imposed, they ultimately turned out to capital's advantage. Employers were forced to abandon the rather primitive approach to profits that depended on lengthening the working day, and turn their attention to raising the productivity of labour. (In Marx's terms, they had to switch their efforts from absolute to relative surplus value.) The result was further and often spectacular improvements in profitability – but left to their own devices, the employers would never have agreed to shortening the working day. It took a major political initiative (and as it happened, one that particularly restricted the employment of women workers) to force them into a new round of economic development. Reshaping employment patterns so that they fit with the new realities of the labour market might well have similar effects; the kind of sexual equality I am describing might then turn out to be compatible with a capitalist economy. It is not compatible, however, with a hands-off non-interventionism that allows the immediate requirements of employers to dictate the hours and patterns of work.

What I am describing here is probably more accurately described as social-democracy than socialism, but it does imply a radically different scale of values in which production is tailored to social need, and caring for people takes equal priority alongside producing marketable goods and services. Socialism in this (rather attenuated) sense is a precondition for sexual equality, for freeing up the opportunities of girls in education or women in employment does not provide the necessary structural changes that can deliver life-long equality, and we need a more decisive challenge to market principles. It is impossible to eliminate all inequalities between people; it is undesirable to eliminate all differences. But both differences and inequalities have to be detached from the accident of being born male or female, so that the choices we make and the inequalities we condone reflect individual, rather than sexual, variation. It was the liberal tradition that first gave voice to this ideal, but it is socialism that could make it reality.

Endnotes

1. First published in *Soundings* (1996) Issue 4, Lawrence and Wishart.

2. Ellen DuBois (1975) "The Radicalism of the Woman Suffrage Movement: Notes Toward the Reconstruction of Nineteenth-Century Feminism" *Feminist Studies* 3, 1/2, p66.

3. For the Owenite approach to these issues, see Barbara Taylor (1983) *Eve and the New Jerusalem*, Virago.

4. First published in 1883, subsequently revised in 1891 and 1895.

5. Written in 1860, published in 1869.

6. J S Mill, "The Subjection of Women", in *Mill Three Essays*, OUP, (1975), p447.

7. *ibid*, p448.

8. First published in 1884.

9. This is largely how I formulated the contrast in an earlier discussion of feminism and equality. See my introduction to Anne Phillips (ed) (1987) *Feminism and Equality*, Basil Blackwell.

10. Cited in Jill Liddington (1984) *The Life and Times of a Respectable Rebel: Selina Cooper 1864-1946*, Virago, p165.

11. Shulamith Firestone (1971) *The Dialectic of Sex*, Jonathan Cape.

12. Ann Snitow (1992) "Feminism and Motherhood: An American Reading" *Feminist Review*, 40.

13. See Pippa Norris "Comparing Legislative Recruitment" in J Lovenduski and P Norris (eds) (1993) *Gender and Party Politics*, Sage.

14. See David Miller's essay in this volume p83-100.

15. See Stuart White's essay in this volume p59-82.

16. For a fuller discussion of the weaknesses of this strategy, see my "Whose Community? Which Individuals?" in D Miliband (ed) (1994) *Reinventing the Left*, Polity Press.

17. *Social Justice: Stragegies for National Renewal* (1994) Vintage, p21.

18. See Stuart White's essay in this volume p59-82.

19. See Ronald Dworkin (1988) "What is Equality? Part 4: Political Equality" *University of San Francisco Law Review*, 22.

20. Robert Nozick (1974) *Anarchy, State and Utopia*, Basil Blackwell.

Equality in a Multicultural Society
Bhikhu Parekh

Broadly speaking and subject to the qualifications to be discussed later, equality implies equal treatment of those judged to be equal in relevant respects. It presupposes a broad agreement on what respects are relevant in a given context, what kind of response is appropriate to them, who are equal in respect to them, and what treatment counts as equal. The agreement is not easy to obtain even in a culturally homogenous society; in multicultural societies it is exceedingly difficult. This paper discusses the kinds of difficulty the concept of equality raises in such societies and the ways in which them might be resolved.

Rather than discuss the question in abstract theoretical terms, or by means of hypothetical and largely unreal examples which rarely capture the complexity and nuances of practical life, I shall examine the real dilemmas different societies have faced and the ways in which they have endeavoured to resolve them, and then briefly draw out their important theoretical implications. For convenience I shall take most of my examples from Britain, and refer to other societies as and when necessary.

Costs and adjustments

Ahmad, a devout Muslim, was employed as a full-time supply teacher by the Inner London Education Authority (ILEA).[1] Initially he taught in a district that was too far from a mosque for him to attend it for the customary Friday afternoon prayer. When he was later transferred to a school that was closer to a mosque, he insisted on attending it every Friday afternoon. This meant that he was absent from the school for the first three-quarters of an hour on Friday afternoons, and had to be covered by other teachers. On ILEA's instructions the head teacher of the school refused to allow him to be absent in this way. When Ahmad declined to comply, ILEA asked him to become a part-time teacher for four and a half days a week. Since that involved a reduction in his salary, he resigned and took the matter to an Industrial Tribunal.

ILEA argued that since Ahmad was unable to meet his contractual obligation to teach on Friday afternoons, it was entitled to ask him to go part-time. It also pointed out that its other Muslim teachers were perfectly happy to forego Friday afternoon prayers, and that Ahmad's absence caused much inconvenience to other teachers and to his pupils. It was argued on Ahmad's behalf that other Muslim teachers' compliance with ILEA's instructions did not affect the validity of his case, for they might not be as devout or courageous as him. It was also argued that all teachers were normally expected to and did, in fact, cover one another, and that Ahmad's contractual obligations could not override his fundamental right to freedom of worship. The Industrial Tribunal dismissed his appeal, a decision later supported by the Employment Appeal Tribunal.

The matter went to the Court of Appeal which, again, rejected his case, but this time by a majority decision. Lord Scarman, who was sympathetic to Ahmad, argued that unlike Jews or Christians, a Muslim's day of prayer fell on a working day and that this placed him at a disadvantage. If a Muslim were not to be given time off for prayer, he would never become a full-time teacher, and that would cause him economic hardship. The educational system therefore had a duty to make suitable arrangements to enable Muslims to attend Friday prayer *even if* that involved extra public expenditure in employing a few more teachers. Since ILEA had failed to do so, Scarman concluded that it had discriminated against Ahmad and treated him unfairly. The other two judges took a different view. Lord Denning, while "upholding religious freedom to the full", argued that Ahmad's insistence on taking time off every Friday on full pay amounted to an unfair plea for "preferential treatment". If Ahmad felt strongly about the Friday prayer, he should bear its cost himself and accept reduction in his salary. As so often happens in a human rights discourse, different judges stressed different rights and reached different conclusions. Lord Scarman emphasised the freedom of worship as guaranteed by Article 9 (1) of the European Convention, while the other two judges stressed Article 9 (2) of the Convention which restricted that freedom in the interest of the rights and freedoms of others. Ahmad went to the European Commission on Human Rights and lost. Ahmad's case raises an important question. A liberal society is committed to the values of equality and fairness. At the same time it has a specific cultural structure and identity which it generally wishes to preserve and which limits its capacity to treat its minorities equally. To ask it radically to restructure its identity in order to accommodate all manner of minority practices is both to be unfair to it and to render collective life unacceptably chaotic and costly. This means that there is a tension at the heart of liberal society. It wishes to maintain its cultural identity, but it also wishes, as a part of its cultural identity, to remove such inequalities and unfairness as its practices cause to its minorities. Since it cannot ignore either demand, it needs to strike a reasonable balance between them. The nature of the balance depends on a number of factors such as the importance of the minority practice to its way of life, the kind, extent and cost of the changes required in the society's way of life, and the society's capacity to make the changes without seriously damaging its coherence and stability. The balance will naturally be struck differently in different societies and by the same society in different contexts. Since it involves a fair and sensitive weighing up of different considerations, the balance cannot be correct or incorrect or even right or wrong but reasonable or unreasonable. Broadly speaking it is reasonable if it takes full account of all the relevant factors, gives each due importance, and can be defended in an open, free and equal debate.

The point becomes clearer if we take the case of Ahmad. Like other British citizens, Ahmad has a right to religious belief and practice, including the right to attend Friday's communal prayer. Unlike Christians whose religious holiday falls on a Sunday, Ahmad's falls on a working day, and he is therefore at a disadvantage. Giving him time off on Friday afternoons removes the disadvantage and is an equalising measure. It does not privilege him, for it neither confers more rights on him nor gives him additional resources to exercise the right he shares with others. Unlike Christians whose religious requirements are met without extra efforts on their part, Muslims need special exemption on Friday afternoons in order to exercise their right of worship. ILEA therefore had a duty to view the demands of Ahmad and other Muslim teachers with the required degree of sympathy, and to do all it could do to cover for their absence. ILEA however, had obligations to its pupils and non-Muslim teachers as well. Its financial resources were limited, and it could not cover for Ahmad and other Muslim teachers if that involved an excessive cost.

The reasonable balance between the conflicting considerations would seem to be that ILEA should have accommodated Ahmad's request by suitably covering for his absence and in return assigning him alternative responsibilities. This need not involve either an additional expenditure or an extra burden on other teachers, for they help out each other in this way all the time as a normal part of their duty. However, even if it did entail some additional cost, ILEA should have undertaken it partly to help Ahmad exercise his right, partly to earn his and other Muslim teacher's goodwill, and partly to send out the message to its non-Muslim staff that it respects religious diversity and is opposed to religious social and other forms of discrimination, an important consideration in a multicultural society not yet free of racism. If the additional cost was excessive, or if ILEA could not release Ahmad because his pupils were unruly, or because other teachers could not be spared, or because he was himself a supply teacher whose whole job was to cover for others, or because this was likely to set a precedent it might not be able to follow in future, or for some other legitimate reason, it could rightly refuse Ahmad's request and ask him to forego his right or bear the cost of exercising it himself by working for only four and a half days a week.

The duty to take full account of others' rights and interests devolves not only on ILEA but also on Ahmad, for he cannot consistently ask it to be reasonable while himself remaining unreasonable. If Friday prayer was flexible, as indeed it is, or if his absence conflicted with others' rights or impeded his school's ability to discharge its obligations to its pupils and their parents, he should not insist on his right, and go to the mosque after school hours as many of his Muslim colleagues did. He cannot insist on exercising his right while expecting others to suspend theirs.

The position I have sketched differs from those taken by the three judges. For Lord Scarman ILEA had a duty to do all that was necessary to accommodate Ahmad. For the other two judges its duty was only limited to making appropriate internal arrangements and excluded incurring any additional cost. The more defensible position would seem to be that ILEA had a duty to go a *reasonable* way towards enabling Ahmad to exercise his right of worship consistently with the rights of other teachers and pupils and the demands on its resources, and that if he asked for more, it was his responsibility to bear the additional cost.

Similar questions have also come up in other countries, and sometimes the courts have taken an excessively narrow view of what constitutes reasonable accommodation of minority employees unable to work on certain days or to do certain kinds of jobs. In *TWA vs Hardison (1977)*, the US Supreme Court held unreasonable any request that involved the slightest additional expenditure or denied other employees their shift and job preferences on some days of the year. This is an excessively restrictive view of the requirements of reasonable accommodation. It takes no account of and makes no attempt to accommodate people with distinct and reasonable religious needs, and virtually denies them certain avenues of employment. It is also unfair because it takes a narrow view of the rights of religious and cultural minorities and a very broad view of those of the rest. One way to deal with such situations might be to build into the employee's employment contract the requirement that they should be prepared to accommodate the reasonable religious and cultural requirements of their fellow-employees.

Accomodating difference

In Ahmad's case the application of the principle of equality became contentious because it required adjustments on the part of his colleagues, affected their rights and those of his pupils, and involved a possible additional cost to his employers. The principle of equality can become hotly contested even when none of these is involved and the question is simply one of tolerating difference.

In 1972, British Parliament passed a law empowering the Minister of Transport to require all motor cyclists to wear crash helmets.[2] When the Minister did so, Sikhs campaigned against it.

One of them broke the law, and was convicted and fined twenty times between 1973 and 1976 for refusing to wear a crash helmet. When he claimed in self-defence that wearing a turban was a religious requirement for him and that he could not replace it with a crash helmet, the presiding judge was unconvinced. He did not challenge the assertion that the turban was a religious requirement for Sikhs, and was content to argue that if for some reason they were unable to wear helmets, they could not ride motor-cycles. In his view the law did not compel people either to wear helmets or to ride motor-cycles, and only required that if they did the latter, they must wear helmets. Since the judge's only concern was to apply the law as it stood, he was correct to argue as he did. Sikhs campaigned against he law with considerable popular support, arguing that the turban was as safe as a crash helmet and that, if they could fight for the British in two world wars without anyone considering their turbans unsafe, they could surely ride motor-cycles. The law was amended in 1976 and exempted them from wearing crash helmets.

The British Parliament was right to amend the law. Its primary purpose was to ensure that people did not die or, since injury is costlier to the state than death, suffer serious injuries riding dangerous vehicles. It hit upon the helmet meeting certain standards as the best safety measure. However the helmet was only contingently related to the basic objective of averting death and injury. If another headgear served the purpose equally well, there was no good reason to disallow it. The helmet was important not in itself but as an embodiment of what the law regarded as the minimum necessary protection. Since the turban largely satisfied that criterion, it was accepted as legally equivalent to the helmet. Although not really a helmet, it became one in law.

This became evident in the subsequent development of the law as it related to Sikhs. The Construction (Head Protection) Regulation 1989 requires all those working on construction sites to wear safety helmets. However the Employment Act 1989, specifically exempts Sikhs, and requires that no employer may refuse to employ them for not agreeing to wear safety helmets. The law grants that exception because it is persuaded by its own scientific tests that the turban offers an acceptable though not equal protection, and is thus legally equivalent to a helmet. An important implication of this argument is that if a turbaned Sikh were to be injured on a construction site as a result of another person's negligence, he would be entitled to claim damages for only such injuries as he would have suffered if he had been wearing a safety helmet. The law is concerned to protect workers on the construction site, and prescribes the helmet as an adequate protection. It takes the helmet as its point of reference in judging other head gears. It does not allow anyone to work on a construction site without an acceptable head gear; on this point it makes no compromises. However, it is willing to compromise on the helmet if two conditions are satisfied. First, the alternative head gear should be shown to offer an equivalent or at least acceptable level of protection. And second, those opting for it should themselves bear the responsibility for such *additional* injury as it may cause. The law lays down the absolute and non-negotiable minimum and uses it to regulate the range of cultural diversity. So far as the minimum requirement is concerned, it places the burden of injury on those causing it. The burden of additional injury is borne by the victims who, for cultural reasons, choose to meet the minimum requirement in their own different ways. Such an arrangement respects differences without violating the principle of equality and accomodates individual choice without placing unequal financial and other burdens on the rest of their fellow citizens.

In Britain, Sikhs in the police and armed forces are entitled to wear turbans, and no one thinks that this is unjust or that it privileges Sikhs. In Canada it has led to a heated debate. Although most major police forces across the country allow Sikhs to wear turbans, the Royal Canadian Mounted Police did not. When it finally decided to allow them, a group of retired officers mounted a strong opposition involving 9,000 letters and a petition signed by 201,000 people. They argued that the RCMP should be, and should be seen to be, free from political and religious bias and that, since the Sikh's turban was a religious symbol, it "undermined the non-religious nature of the force" and violated other Canadians' "constitutional right to a secular state free of religious symbols". Furthermore since Sikhs insisted on wearing the turban, their demand implied that they valued their religion far more than their police duties. In the eyes of the critics, Canada had taken its multiculturalism too far and should insist on the traditional Stetson. The matter went to the Trial Division of the Federal Court of Canada, which ruled that the objection to the turban was "quite speculative and vague", and that the turban did not compromise the non-religious character of the RCMP. Three retired officers of the RCMP appealed to the Supreme Court, which dismissed the appeal and upheld the Sikh's right to wear the turban.

Although the objection against the turban smacks of cultural intolerance and treats Sikhs unequally, it is not wholly devoid of merit. The RCMP is a powerful and much cherished national symbol and, since Canada has few national symbols, there is something to be said for retaining the Stetson. However, one could argue that precisely because the RCMP is a national symbol, it should allow the turban to symbolise the country's officially endorsed multicultural identity. Furthermore, several provincial forces as well as the Canadian Courts and House of Commons allow Sikhs to wear turbans with no suggestion that this compromises the discharge of their official duties, diminishes their loyalty to the state, or detracts from the country's secular character. There is no reason why the RCMP should be different. Besides, wearing a turban does not signify that the wearer values his religion more than his professional integrity, nor does his replacing it with a Stetson indicate the opposite. Pushed to its logical conclusion, the criticism of the turban would imply that those wearing the traditional Stetson are likely to be partial to whites and hostile to others. One would therefore have to replace the Stetson with a cultural neutral head gear, which would have the double disadvantage of satisfying neither the Sikhs nor the whites and leaving the basic problem unsolved. Again, it is not at all true that Canada is committed to a narrow and bland form of secularism. If it were, it would have to change its coat-of-arms, disallow prayer in the Federal parliament, expunge reference to God in the swearing-in ceremony of Cabinet ministers, and so on. Since opponents of the turban are unsympathetic to these changes, their objection is clearly specious and discriminatory.

The diversity of head dress has raised problems in other societies as well, especially in relation to the armed forces and the police, the symbols and protectors of national identity. Simcha Goldman, an orthodox rabbi serving in the secular capacity of a clinical psychologist in the US Air Force, was asked to resign when he refused to stop wearing his yarmulke which the Air Force decided was against its standard dress requirement. When the matter reached the supreme court, it upheld 5-4 the decision of the Air Force.[3] Shortly thereafter the Ninth Circuit Court of Appeals, basing its decision on the Goldman case, upheld the Army's right to refuse to process the enlistment application of a Sikh whose turban did not conform to its dress requirements.[4] When the ban on the yarmulke was widely criticised, the Secretary of State argued that the uniforms of the armed forces were "cherished symbols of service, pride, history and traditions", and that allowing variations in them was bound to "operate to the detriment of order and discipline", foster "resentment and divisiveness", "degrade unit cohesion", and to reduce combat effectiveness.[5] The Supreme Court decision rightly outraged many members of Congress, which by a sizeable majority asked the armed forces to introduce greater flexibility in their dress codes.

There is much to be said in favour of uniforms in the armed forces. Since the armed forces are closely identified with the state and symbolise its unity, uniforms reinforce the consciousness of their national role and create corporate ethos and identity. And it goes without saying that they should be suitable for combat. However, all this has to be balanced against other equally relevant considerations. If the yarmulke, turban and other religious head dresses were to be disallowed, Jews, Sikhs and others would be denied both an avenue of employment and an opportunity to serve their country. Furthermore, the United States is a culturally diverse society made up of people of different religious faiths. There is no obvious reason why its national symbols, including military uniforms, should not reflect that fact. Besides if differences of mere head dress are likely to detract from collective solidarity and unit cohesion, the differences of colour, accent and facial features are likely to do so even more, and we would have to ban blacks, Jews, Asians and others from joining the armed forces. All this means that while the uniform should not be discarded, it should be open to appropriate modification to accommodate genuine religious, cultural and other requirements, provided of course that they do not compromise military effectiveness.

The controversy concerning uniforms occurs in civilian areas of life as well, where it raises issues that are at once both similar and different. Since no question of national unity or symbolism is involved, the controversy has only a local significance. However, it involves far more people, usually women, and affects their life chances to a much greater degree.

Many Asian women's refusal to wear uniforms in hospitals, stores and schools has led to much litigation and contradictory judgements in Britain. A Sikh woman who, on qualifying as a nurse, intended to wear her traditional dress of a long skirt (quemiz) over baggy trousers (shalwar) rather than the required uniform, was refused a training place on a nursing course by her Health Authority. The Industrial Tribunal upheld her complaint on the ground that since her traditional dress was a cultural requirement and did not impede the discharge of her duties, requiring her to replace it with a uniform was unjustified. The tribunal was overruled by the Employment Appeal Tribunal, which took the opposite and much criticised view. Since rules about nurses' uniforms are laid down by the General Nursing Council, the latter promptly intervened under government pressure and made more flexible rules. This enabled the Health Authority to offer the Sikh woman a place on the nursing course on the understanding that as a qualified nurse her trousers should be grey and the shirt white.[6]

Cases involving bans on traditional dresses, beards, etc. have occurred in schools, stores and other public places as well, and have led to contradictory judgements. Sometimes the courts took one view, and were overruled on appeal. The discrepancy arose because they used two different criteria in deciding such cases. Sometimes the courts asked if the job requirements were plausible or understandable, that is, if "good reasons" could be given for them. On other occasions they thought that such a criterion justified almost everything, and insisted that the job requirement should be objectively necessary, that is, they should be indispensable for the jobs concerned and there should be no alternative ways of doing the job. It sounds plausible to say that surgeons or those working in chocolate factories should shave off their beards, for loose hairs could easily cause infection or pose a risk to public health. On closer examination the requirement turns out to be objectively unnecessary, for beards do not mean loose hair and, if necessary, they can always be covered by suitable clothing. After all, we do not ask people in these jobs to shave hair of their heads and arms. Although the test of objective necessity is reasonable, it runs the risk of taking a purely instrumental view of the job requirements and stripping the organisations concerned and the prevailing way of life of their cultural identity. Take the case of hospital nurses' uniforms. One could argue that since the uniforms are not objectively necessary for doing the required medical tasks, anyone may wear anything. This is to miss the crucial point that the uniform symbolises and reinforces the ethos and self-conception of the organisation, is a highly visible and concentrated expression of the collective spirit of the nursing profession, structures the expectations and behaviour of their patients, and so on. The instrumental view of rationality implicit in the test of objective necessity is also likely to provoke resentment against the minorities, whose demands might be seen to undermine a much-cherished tradition. It is also unjust because, while it respects the cultural identity of the minority, it ignores that of the wider community. The concept of objective necessity should therefore be defined in a culturally sensitive manner, and should do justice to both the minority and the established ways of life. This means that uniforms should be kept in hospitals, schools and wherever else they are part of the tradition, but should be open to appropriate adjustments. Such cultural accommodation neither deculturalises the organisations concerned and renders them bland, nor eclectically multiculturalises them and renders them comical. Instead it reconciles the prevailing tradition with minority values and practices, both preserves and adapts the tradition to changing circumstances and facilitates minority integration into the suitably opened up mainstream society.

Relevant respects

As we saw earlier equality requires, among other things, that those who are equal in relevant respects should be treated equally. In the cases discussed so far, it was relatively easy to identify which respects were relevant and of what the equal treatment consisted. In a culturally diverse society, situations sometimes arise when it becomes difficult to decide which respects are *relevant,* whether two individuals belonging to different cultures are *equal* in respect to them, and what counts as their equal *treatment.* I shall take each of these in turn.

In Britain as in all western and many non-western societies, the law lays down that a marriage is void if it is contracted under duress, a concept not easy to define in a culturally neutral manner. A British Asian girl, who had married her parentally chosen husband because of the threat of ostracism by her family, asked the court to annul her marriage on grounds of duress. The court declined, arguing that this would not have amounted to duress for a white British girl, and that duress only occurred when there was a "threat of imminent danger to life and liberty." This was a culturally insensitive interpretation of duress and was rightly criticised. Not surprisingly the court did a complete *volte face* a few years later in deciding the case of another Asian girl, It took the view that although acute social pressure did not amount to duress for a white British girl, it did so for her Asian counterpart, and declared her marriage void.

The Asian girl is clearly treated differently, raising the question whether the difference amounts to privilege on her part. *Prima facie,* it would seem that she is offered an additional ground for dissolution of marriage, and is thus privileged. However, this is not the case. Equality requires that those who are equal in relevant respects should be treated equally. The law lays down that free choice or absence of duress is the basis of a valid marriage. Since ostracism by the family virtually amounts to social death and hence to duress in Asian society in a way it does not in white British society, the differential treatment of the Asian and white girls does not offend against the principle of equality. It does not give the Asian girl a new ground for divorce, but interprets the existing ground in a culturally sensitive manner.

Sometimes the recognition of cultural difference does involve unequal rights. Take the case of Sikhs who are allowed by the law to carry a suitably covered *kirpan* (a small dagger) in public places on the ground that this is a mandatory symbol of their religion. If other citizens asked to be allowed to carry a *kirpan*, their request would be turned down on the ground that the right is given only to those for whom carrying it is a religions requirements. Short of religious conversion, they cannot acquire that right. This raises the question of whether non-Sikhs can legitimately complain of discrimination or unequal treatment. There is no discrimination involved both because their religious requirements are not ignored, and because they do not suffer adversely as a result of the law respecting those of the Sikhs. As for the complaint of inequality, there *is* a *prima facie* inequality of rights in the sense that Sikhs can do what others cannot. However the alleged inequality grows out of the requirements of the principle of equal respect for all, and is not so much inequality as an appropriate translation of that principle in a different religious context. When a Muslim is allowed time off for communal prayer on Friday afternoons but not a Sikh, the latter cannot legitimately complain of inequality. Since their religious requirements are different, their equal right to religion entails different treatment. In deciding whether two individuals or communities are treated equally, we need to consider not what specific actions they are or are not able to undertake, but whether these are derived from a more general right which they both equally enjoy and which is concretised differently in their cases. This is like two individuals who both enjoy the right to equal medical attention but who receive different treatment depending on the nature of their illness.

Equal in relevant respects

Sometimes we know what respect is relevant in a given context, but find it difficult to decide if two individuals are equal in respect to it. Take *l'affaire du foulard* which first surfaced in France in September 1989 and has haunted it ever since.[7] Three Muslim girls from North Africa, two of them sisters, wore the *hijab* (head scarf) to their ethnically mixed school in Creil, some sixty kilometres north of Paris. In the previous year, twenty Jewish students had refused to attend classes on Saturday mornings and autumn Friday afternoons when the Sabbath arrived before the close of the school, and the headmaster had refused to compromise. Worried about the trend of events, he objected to the Muslim girls wearing the *hijab* in the classroom on the grounds that it went against the *laicité* of the French state schools. Since the girls refused to comply, he barred them from attending the school. As a gesture of solidarity many Muslim girls throughout France began to wear *hijabs* to school and the matter acquired national importance. The Education Minister, Lionel Jospin, consulted the Conseil d'Etat which ruled that the *hijab* did not violate the principle of *laicité*, provided that the girls did not engage in "pressure, provocation, proselytism or propaganda", the decision on which was to be made by the local education authority on a case-by-case basis. The vagueness of the ruling not only failed to give the headmaster clear guidance but publicly revealed the ambiguities of the official policy. Soon there were more incidents of *hijab* wearing and protests by Muslims, provoking counter protests by secular Frenchmen. The stand-off was finally resolved when one of the girls voluntarily, and the other two under pressure from King Hassan of Morocco, agreed to drop the scarves to the shoulders in the classroom. The issue flared up again in September 1994 when the principal of a middle school in Nantua barred two girls from the school for wearing the *hijab*. The Education Minister Francois Bayrou ruled that while wearing discreet religious symbols was acceptable, ostentatious symbols which in themselves constituted elements of proselytism or discrimination were unacceptable, and that the *hijab* fell under that category. Head scarves were now banned as a matter of public policy and school decisions to the contrary were declared void.

The national debate on the *hijab* went to the heart of the French conceptions of citizenship and national identity, and divided the country. Several intellectuals of the left expressed the dominant view when in a letter to *Le Nouvel Observateur* they urged the government not to perpetrate the "Munich of Republican Education" and asked the teachers not to "capitulate". For them, as for a large body of Frenchmen, France was a one and indivisible nation based on a single culture. To be its citizen was to transcend, indeed to shed, one's ethnic and other cultural particularities and to be assimilated into the French culture. Every French citizen stood in a direct and unmeditated relationship with the French nation and enjoyed equality with the rest. Unlike the ethnically obsessed "Anglo Saxons" who cherish "the right to be different" and end up ghettoising their minorities and fragmenting their nations, France recognised no ethnic minorities and rejected all forms of ethnic and religious self-consciousness. As Jean-Claude Basseau, former head of the French Office of International Migrations and advisor to Pasque, put it "When someone emigrates, he does not simply change country, he also changes history. Foreigners arriving in France must understand that their ancestors are the Gauls. They have a new fatherland".

For the majority of Frenchmen, the school was the central tool of assimilation into the French culture and could not conceivably tolerate ethnic self-expressions. The *hijab* was particularly objectionable because it symbolised both a wholly alien culture and the subordinate status of women. Wearing it implied a refusal to become French, to integrate, to be like the rest. Since *laicité* was a hard won principle of long historical standing, the French state could not compromise with it without damaging its identity. As Serge July, the editor of *Liberation,* put it, ".. behind the scarf is the question of immigration, behind immigration is the debate over integration, and behind integration the question of *laicité*".

A small but influential body of French writers took a different view. Danielle Mitterand, the President's wife, observed, "if today, two hundred years after the revolution, the secular schools cannot welcome all religions in France, all forms of expression, that means there has been a setback". Alain Goldmann, the Chief Rabbi of Paris, supported the wearing of head scarves, saying that "acquainting little French children with 'difference' is an excellent pedagogical technique. They learn to know and respect others". Several liberal and anti-racist spokesmen argued that French unity should be grounded in a recognition rather than denial of differences, and that the state school's *laicité* should be broadly interpreted to make room for minority cultures. Thanks to such views which had been gaining ground for the past few years, France had witnessed the *droit à la différence* movement in the early 1980s and the *vivre Ensemble* campaign of the mid 1980s, both of which celebrated diversity, encouraged the teaching of mother tongues in schools, and fostered a less assimilationist view of education and

French national identity. Although the assimilationist view eventually triumphed in the *hijab* controversy, the pluralist view not only received a respectful hearing but also won a few converts.

The principal argument against allowing Muslim girls to wear the *hijab* was that it violated the principle of *laicité*, an essential component of French national identity, and was thus incompatible with the French self-understanding. Although the argument is not conclusive, for national identity is a historical product and needs to be redefined when the circumstances including the social composition of the country change, it would have a considerable force if the French education system had lived up to the principle of *laicité*. This was not in fact the case. France not only allows but publicly funds Catholic schools where *laicité* is obviously not a value. More to the point, state schools allow Catholic girls to wear the cross and other insignia of religious identity. Muslim spokesmen argued that allowing the cross but not the *hijab* was discriminatory and amounted to unequal treatment.

Defenders of the ban, including the Minister of Education, rejected the Muslim charge of discrimination on the ground that the *hijab* was not equivalent to the cross, and that the two groups of girls were not equal in relevant respects. First, unlike the "discreetly" worn cross, the "ostentatious" *hijab* was intended to put pressure on other Muslim girls, and entailed "proselytisation". Secondly, unlike the freely worn cross, the *hijab* symbolised and reinforced women's oppression. It was worn under parental and social pressure and perpetuated Muslim patriarchy. Thirdly, unlike the unselfconsciously worn cross, the *hijab* was a politically and ideologically motivated assertion of religious identity inspired by the rise of fundamentalism among French Muslims and their home countries.

Although there is a good deal of humbug, misplaced anxiety and false alarm in these arguments, they are not totally devoid of substance. Both the cross and the *hijab* are religious symbols, and hence bases of equal claims. However, religious symbols cannot be defined and compared in the abstract, for they acquire different meanings and symbolise different things in different contexts, and might sometimes even cease to be religious in nature. We need to contextualise them and to compare them not abstractly or "in themselves" but in terms of the character and significance they might have acquired at a particular point in time. The question is not whether the *hijab* is the Islamic equivalent of the Christian cross, but whether, in contemporary France, wearing the *hijab* has a broadly similar religious significance to wearing the cross. We cannot therefore dismiss the ban in the name of an abstract right to equality of religious freedom; instead we need to take seriously the three arguments made in support of it and assess their validity.

As for the first argument, the *hijab* is certainly visible even perhaps ostentatious, but there is no evidence to support the view that it was intended to proselytise among non-Muslims or to put religious pressure on other Muslim girls beyond the minimum that is inherent in the wearing of religious symbols. Conversely the cross is not necessarily discreet for Catholic girls do sometimes display and even flaunt and talk about it, and it is clearly visible when they engage in sports, swimming and such other activities.

The second argument which contrasts the freely worn cross with the coerced *hijab* is no more persuasive. It privileges choices by adolescent girls and disapproves of parental pressure. There is no good reason to accept this biased view. Indeed if we did, we would have to ask if pupils had chosen their subjects or careers and were working hard, engaging in extra-curricular activities and so on, freely or under parental pressure, and to disallow all that fell under the latter. Even if we accepted the distinction between choice and coercion, the argument would remain suspect. We have no means of knowing that wearing the cross was a free choice by the girls involved and not done under parental or church pressure. Conversely we have no means of knowing that Muslim girls wore the *hijab* under parental or communal pressure. It was true that they had hitherto avoided it. However, it is quite possible that they now defined their identity differently or felt more confident about expressing it. Indeed the father of the two Creil girls said that the decision to wear the *hijab* was theirs and that he had been trying to convince them out of it. Since he might be saying this under pressure or to avoid embarrassment, we might refer to the remark of a young girl who was inspired by the three Creil girls to start wearing the head scarf in 1994: "I feel completely liberated by the veil. As soon as I put it on, I felt as if I'd blossomed. The veil allows a women no longer to be a slave to her body. It is the belief that a woman can go far through means other than using her body".

This means that the third argument for the ban is unconvincing, for wearing the *hijab* need not be a form of ideologically based self-assertion. As for the fears about the rise of fundamentalism, a term that was never clearly defined, they were speculative and irrelevant to the argument. Only three out of scores of Muslim girls had worn the *hijab*, and the father of two of them had not only no history of religious activism but was positively embarrassed by the publicity. There was not much evidence that most of the French Muslim Community was becoming religiously militant. Some of them did show sympathy for traditional values, but that was their choice, was shared by many sections of the mainstream French society as well, and hardly amounted to fundamentalist militancy.

The issues raised by the *hijab* are not confined to France. In Britain, the state funds thousands of religious schools, but it has constantly rejected Muslim requests for similar schools on one flimsy ground or another.[8] Its real reasons, often stated in private and sometimes hinted at in public, are mainly two. First, the state funds religious schools because it expects that in addition to grounding their pupils into the basic principles of their religion, they will also develop their analytical and critical faculties, provide secular knowledge, and prepare them for life in a democratic and secular society. This is a difficult balance to strike, which non-Muslim religious schools have been able to achieve after a long struggle. Since Muslim schools are bound to become nurseries of reactionary and militant ideas in the current fundamentalist phase of Islam, they are unlikely to achieve the basic objectives of education and may rightly be disallowed. Secondly, state funding of religious schools in Britain is the result of specific historical circumstances. British society now realises that such schools are undesirable. Since it cannot renege on its past commitments to existing schools, it can at least stop perpetuating the problem by refusing to fund new ones.

Opponents of Muslim schools therefore argue that no inequality is involved in denying state funding to Muslim schools while continuing to provide it to other religious schools. Equality requires that equal treatment be given to those who are equal in relevant respects. The relevant respect here is the capacity to provide a balanced religious education. Since Muslim schools lack the capacity, they cannot be treated on a par with other religious schools. The second argument has a different thrust. It does not say anything about whether or not the two kinds of schools are equal in relevant respects. Rather it asserts that the state has decided to change its policy on funding religious schools. Since it cannot abrogate its past commitments, it must continue to fund Christian and Jewish schools. Although this involves treating Muslims unequally, such inequalities are inherent in social life and cannot be avoided. Long-established groups often enjoy rights based on past commitments and policies. When the policies are changed, they retain the rights which are no longer available to their successors.

Opponents of state funding for Muslim schools make the important theoretical point that equality should not be understood in purely formal and abstract terms. Just because some religious communities enjoy state-funded schools, it does not *necessarily* follow that denying them to Muslims amounts to inequality, for they might not be able to fulfil the socially prescribed objectives of education or the state might sincerely wish to discontinue such schools. Rather than accuse their opponents of being anti-Muslim, racists, *et cetera*, on the basis of an abstract and untenable view of inequality, we need to see if their two arguments have any merit.

Their first argument is suspect. To say that Islam is currently going through a fundamentalist phase is a gross exaggeration, true at best of some and not of all Muslim countries. More to the point, it is not at all true of British Islam. Since the British government allows privately funded Muslim schools, it evidently shares this scepticism, and is wrong to raise the bogey of fundamentalism only when state funding is involved. There is also a rise in Christian fundamentalism, but the British government shows no signs of closing down or issuing suitable warnings to state-funded Christian schools. Furthermore, the government enjoys the right to inspect and regulate schools, especially their curriculum, pedagogy and general ethos, and has enough power to counter such forms of fundamentalism as might arise in Muslim schools. The power is bound to be greater, and its exercise more acceptable, if the state also funds them. The second argument is no better. The British state certainly has the right to change its policy on funding religious schools. This involves not only denying state funding to new schools, but also phasing out the existing ones over a mutually agreed period of time, something which the British state shows not the slightest sign of doing. There is no evidence either that it is putting pressure on them to become secular or even to reduce the religious content of the curriculum. Since neither of the two arguments advanced by the government is valid, the denial of state funds to Muslim schools amounts to unequal treatment.

In the light of our discussions of the *hijab* controversy in France and the state funding of Muslim schools in Britain, it should be clear that equality between cultures is logically different from and cannot be understood along the lines of equality between individuals. Unlike the latter, it is deeply embedded in and inseparable from the wider cultural and political relations between the communities involved. And the cultural communities often contain a wide variety of views on a subject and cannot be homogenised and reified. The case for intercultural equality should not be made in such highly abstract and historical terms that it ignores genuine differences between communities involved or fails to address the deepest anxieties of the wider society. I suggest that we should take a contextualised view of equality, identify what respects are really relevant, and demand equal treatment of those shown to be equal in these respects. If the *hijab* really is different from the cross, which it is not, then Muslim girls may legitimately be denied the right to wear it without incurring the charge of inequality. And if Muslim schools do really run the risk that their critics fear, which they do not, or if the British state does really wish to discontinue religious schools, which it does not, then they may legitimately be denied state funding without offending against the principle of equality.

Taking such a contextualised, politically and historically sensitive, and nuanced view of equality, no doubt, creates its own problems. We leave too much space for specious reasoning, alarmist fears and political inertia, and we also run the risk of not knowing how to compare differences, how to separate relevant from irrelevant differences, how to assess the context, and so on. It is therefore tempting to take the more dependable route of insisting on the general right of equality, and to argue that since Christians and Jews have a right to their schools, Muslims too must have a right to state-funded schools. If what I have said is correct, the temptation should be resisted. If we ask the law to take such a mechanical and simplistic view of equality, then we cannot consistently ask it to take cultural differences into account in the case of Ahmad, the Sikhs and the marriage of the Asian girl discussed earlier, and that would obviously lead to injustice. The question therefore is not whether Muslims have a right to religious freedom but what, if anything, that right entails in a specific context, and that involves deciding what features of the context are relevant and whether Muslims are equal in respect to them. The movement from a general right to equality to the right to a specific treatment in a specific context, that is, from a general right to religion to the right to wear the *hijab* in a school, is not direct and deductive but contextually mediated. It is not therefore enough to appeal to the general right to equality. One also needs to show that there is equality in the relevant features of the context and that it entails identical treatment.

As we saw, once we move away from the simple assertion of the right to equality and take a contextualised view of it, we are obviously open to the danger of alarmist fears and dishonest and racist reasoning with the consequent injustice to minorities. The French ban on the *hijab* and the British denial of publicly funded Muslim schools were at least in part motivated by anti-Muslim sentiments, and we need to guard against this. One way to do this is to insist that equality requires identical treatment and to place the onus of justification on those seeking to depart from it. Thus British Muslims would be assumed to be entitled to state-funded schools and it would be up to the government to prove to the satisfaction of all concerned why such schools might be denied to them.

We might go further and allow the unconvinced minorities to appeal to the courts against the decisions of the government. Part of the reason why British Muslims continue to feel bitter has to do with the fact that there is no appeal against the government's decision, and hence no opportunity to challenge its reasons and to expose its prejudices. Another measure would be to develop a suitable public forum where such complex issues can be debated between the representatives of different communities. The kind of consultative forum that the French have developed is a good example of this.

Equal treatment

Sometimes it is difficult to decide what constitutes equal treatment because several different forms of treatment fit that description. England has long had an established church, which enjoys rights not available to other religions. Twenty six Anglican bishops sit in the House of Lords; the Church of England alone has the right to officiate at such state ceremonies as coronation and royal weddings and to perform pastoral duties in the armed forces; the reigning monarch is the "defender of the faith", and their children must marry only the Protestants, and so on. England also has a law proscribing blasphemy against Christianity.

In the aftermath of the Rushdie affair in 1989, British Muslims began to complain that these arrangements privileged Christianity and treated non-Christian religions unequally.[9] The complaint received two very different responses. Some, mainly the conservatives, rejected it on the ground that since Britain was both a Christian *society* in the sense that Christianity meant much to most of its citizens and was a source of many of their moral values, and a Christian *state* in the sense that a historical settlement between the state and the Church of England had made Christianity an integral part of the former's corporate identity, Christianity rightly enjoyed a privileged status. Being woven into the very structure of British national identity, it could not and should not be treated as just one religion among many. Others, mainly but not only the liberals, conceded the Muslim charges of discrimination and inequality, but responded in two different ways. Most of them agreed that the principle of equality required disestablishment of the Anglican church, but disagreed about the anti-blasphemy law. Some favoured the abolition, whereas others urged its extension to all religions, arguing that either course of action fully respected the demands of the principle of religious equality.

Muslim spokesmen rejected the conservative argument on three grounds. First, no historical settlement could claim permanence. It was a product of its time and subject to revision in the light of new circumstances. Secondly, taken to the logical conclusion, such a positivist argument justified all manner of existing privileges and practices and denied justice to newcomers. Thirdly, the principle of equality, which Britain claimed to uphold, required that all religions should be treated equally, irrespective of their age, history and membership.

As for the liberal argument, Muslim leaders endorsed the extension of the anti-blasphemy law but not its abolition. If the Church of England did not need the protection of the law, it did not have to avail of it, but there was no reason to deny it to those in need of it. Furthermore abolition of the anti-blasphemy law granted Muslims negative or formal but not positive or real equality; indeed since there was a vast inequality of power and status between the two religious communities, the abolition was likely to make no difference to the securely established Christianity but bound to have disproportionately adverse effects on minority religions. Muslim spokesmen also argued that their religion was under particular threat in the current climate, and that it was perfectly fair to grant special protection to the weak. After all, the anti-discrimination legislation, which singled out women and ethnic minorities for special protection, was based on that principle, and so at a different level was the welfare state.

We then have four different interpretations of the concept of equal treatment of all religions. First, the state is not to persecute or suppress any religion but may rightly privilege one that happens to be an integral part of its history and identity. Second, it should protect all religions equally. Third, it should not institutionalise and protect any religion. And fourth, it should protect one under threat in the same way that it grants extra protection to individuals under threat or in special need. This raises the question as to which of these four is the "correct" or rather the most reasonable interpretation of the principle of religious equality. The question is not easy to answer. If we define the principle in terms of equal formal rights, only the second and third interpretations qualify, and do so equally. If we define it in terms of equal outcome or equally effective protection of all religions, then the second and the fourth but not the third would qualify. In either case the first interpretation would seem grossly discriminatory and would have to be rejected.

The discussion is further complicated by the fact that religious equality is an ambiguous concept. It could mean equal respect for religions taken as *collective wholes,* or equal respect for the religious beliefs and practices of all *individuals;* that is, it could mean either equality *of* religions or equal right *to* religion. In the first sense of the term, all but the first of the four interpretations mentioned above satisfy the principle of equality; in the second sense, the first interpretation not only qualifies but might even have an edge over the others. Once the religious beliefs of all individuals are equally respected, which the first interpretation secures, no apparent injustice is done to minorities if the religion of the overwhelming majority of the citizens is given *some* precedence over others. This is especially so when that precedence has been long enjoyed, is built into the very structure of the state, and has no apparent adverse effects on religious minorities.

Since both equality in general and religious equality in particular can be differently defined, all four interpretations are valid in their own different ways. None can be declared illegitimate or unreasonable on the basis of an essentialist or allegedly "true" conception of equality. How then can we choose between them? We obviously need to step outside the narrow and formal discussion of equality, and take into account such external but highly relevant factors as the context of its application, other political values that are just as important as if not more important than equality, and the character of the political system.

As we saw, religious equality means equality of right *to* religion or equality *of* religions. The former is beyond dispute in a liberal society, which should give all its citizens equal rights to religions beliefs and practices. The second kind of equality is not so simple. Like all other societies Britain has a distinct history, traditions, way of life, and so forth, and hence a specific cultural character that makes it the kind of society it is and distinguishes it from others. Among other things it is profoundly shaped by Christianity, as is evident in its moral life, myths, political and moral discourse, literature, art and self-conception. Since Britain cannot leap out of its cultural skin, to deny the Christian component of its identity in the name of granting equal status to all its religions is unjust because it denies the bulk of its citizens their history, and is likely to provoke widespread resentment. It is also dangerous because when sentiments and sensibilities that are deeply inscribed in the way of life of a community are denied legitimate public expressions, they often tend to reappear at other levels in ugly forms.

While all this is true, it is equally true that Britain has undergone marked demographic changes in recent decades. It now has a sizeable number of religious minorities with their own distinct histories and traditions, about which they feel just as strongly as the rest of the British citizens do about theirs. The minorities are an integral part of British society, and deserve not only equal religious and other rights but also an official acknowledgement of their presence in both the symbols of the state and the dominant definition of national identity. The acknowledgement cannot be equal, not so much because the minority religious communities are numerically unequal as because they have not shaped the British identity as decisively as Christianity has, are not an equally deep and pervasive presence in British political culture, and do not form an integral and central part of British society as does Christianity. As individuals, all British citizens should have equal religious rights because they are equal in relevant respects. However, they have not played an equal part in shaping, and are not equally central to, the country's national identity. Since they are not equal in *this* respect, they cannot demand *equal* recognition in its self-understanding and self-definition, nor complain of inequality or injustice when equal public recognition is denied them. They are, however, an integral part of British society and deserve and can rightly demand *some* public recognition by the British state.

Any reasonable interpretation of religious equality understood as equality of religions must take account of both these facts, and reconcile the equally legitimate demands of Britain's historical identity and the principle of equality, of both the majority and the minorities. None of the four interpretations mentioned earlier does this. The first stresses the importance of identity but ignores the demands of equality; the other three do the opposite in their own different ways. The only way to reconcile the two demands is both to accept the privileged state of Christianity *and* to give public recognition to other religions. Christianity may therefore rightly remain the central component of British collective identity, but other religions must also receive adequate, though not necessarily equal, recognition and representation in the institutions, rituals and ceremonies of the state. Along with the Anglican bishops, representatives of other religions could be appointed to the House of Lords; state ceremonies such as the coronation and the remembrance day could have a non-Christian component; the monarch could patronise non-Christian festivals and events; and so on. In so doing British society both retains its historically acquired religious identity and publicly acknowledges its current multi-religious composition. Britain may, of course decide to disestablish the Anglican church, but that is an altogether different matter and is not required by the principle of religious equality. *So long as* it retains the established church, it may legitimately privilege Christianity provided that other religions receive their due.

As for the anti-blasphemy law, it is only contingently related to the established church. In an earlier era the two went together; in today's freer climate they need not. They can therefore be uncoupled, and the anti-blasphemy law discussed separately. As we saw there are four possible ways of dealing with it, namely, to keep it as it is, to abolish it, to extend it to all religions, or to protect only the religion under threat. Anti-blasphemy law relates to people's religious beliefs and practices and seeks to protect them against scurrilous, abusive or offensive attacks. It pertains to the right *to* religion rather than *of* religions. Since the religious beliefs and practices of all citizens deserve equal respect, the first alternative which privileges Christianity is discriminatory and deserves to be rejected. The fact that Christianity is the religion of the majority or central to national identity is relevant in other contexts but not in this one, for here we are concerned with civil rights and not with the political expression of national identity. Since every religion can claim to be under threat and since we have no means of adjudicating these claims in a collectively acceptable manner, the fourth alternative is also ruled out. This leaves us with the second and third alternatives. Since Christianity enjoys cultural and political pre-eminence, and since minority religions are relatively powerless, abolition of the anti-blasphemy law has a disproportionately adverse effect on them. Unless there are other reasons for abolishing the law, the third interpretation that it should be extended to all religions has most to be said in favour of it.

The anti-blasphemy law cannot, of course, be discussed in isolation from the larger questions about the place of religion in public life and the state's relation to it. If we took the view that religion has no role in public life or is not a desirable institution or is of no concern to the state, then the anti-blasphemy law should be abolished. If, on the other hand, we took the view that religion has an important contribution to make to public life, that its voice needs to be heard along with secular and other voices, that it should be subjected to the discipline of public debate rather than left to sulk or be manipulated. by irresponsible leaders, and so on, then the state would need to respect and guard it against pointless and abusive attacks. Whether or not to retain the anti-blasphemy law depends on our answers to these and related questions. And it is only when we have answered them that the principle of equality becomes operative.

Implications

In the previous sections I have discussed specific cases and highlighted both the kinds of problems the principle of equality raises in a culturally diverse society and the ways in which they might be resolved. It would be useful to conclude by drawing out some of the general theoretical implications of our discussion.

Almost from its very beginning Western political thought has been preoccupied with the question of equality, and has given rise to an unusually rich and varied discourse on the subject. The discourse, however, has suffered from one major weakness. Since most writers either ignored the importance of culture or assumed a culturally homogenous society, their discussions of equality lacked cultural sensitivity. Although they discussed the legal, civil, political and other rights of citizens, they rarely discussed the question of cultural rights in the twofold sense of the individual's right *to* culture and rights *of* cultures or rather cultural communities.

With such exceptions as Herder and the Romantics, hardly anyone has explored what, if any, cultural rights citizens can justifiably demand and whether cultural communities can be bearers of rights. Furthermore, although political thinkers discussed equality of individuals, they paid little attention to the question of equality of cultural communities. They asked whether, why and within what limits all human beings or citizens should be treated equally, but did not raise these questions in relation to cultures. Again, although they developed a large vocabulary around the idea of equality including such concepts as equal consideration, equal respect, equal treatment, equality of opportunity, equal rights and equality before the law, they generally analysed these concepts in the context of a culturally homogenous society. As a result their analysis does not readily apply to discussions of inter-cultural equality and has only a limited value in dealing with the problems of multicultural societies. In this paper, I have briefly sketched how we might go about constructing a culturally sensitive theory of equality.

Since human beings are culturally embedded, such concepts as equal respect for persons, equal opportunity and equality before the law need to be interpreted in a culturally sensitive manner. Unless we appreciate that human beings need to be located against their cultural backgrounds, and their actions interpreted in terms of the systems of meaning characteristic of their cultures, we misunderstand them and do them injustice. Indeed in assimilating them to our system of meaning, we deny their distinctive identity and can hardly be said to respect them. For example, it was recently discovered that ethnic minority candidates for jobs were systematically underscored and rejected because their habit of not looking their interviewers in the eye led the latter to conclude that they were shifty and devious and likely to prove unreliable. By failing to appreciate that the candidates belonged to a different culture from theirs and needed to be understood in terms of it, the interviews ended up treating them unequally with their white competitors.

Like the concept of equal respect, that of equal opportunity also needs to be interpreted in a culturally sensitive manner.[10] Opportunity is a subject-dependent concept in the sense that a facility, a resource, or a course of action is just a mute and passive possibility and not an *opportunity* for an individual if she lacks the capacity, the cultural disposition, or the necessary cultural knowledge and resources to take advantage of it. And similarly a course of action is not an *option* to her if it does not form part of her view of the world and is morally or culturally too costly. As we saw, a Sikh is abstractly or "in principle" free to send his son to a school that disallows a turban, but for all practical purposes the school is closed to him. Requiring the orthodox Jew to give up his yarmulke, or the Hindu or Muslim women to wear skirts, in order to be eligible for certain kinds of jobs is to close these avenues of employment to them. The capacity involved here is cultural in nature and, since in some cases it is bound up with the individual's sense of identity, it sometimes has the same force as a physical disability. In a culturally diverse society, equal opportunity requires that the available options should be more or less equally acceptable to members of different communities. Amartya Sen's otherwise useful concept of individual capability is defined in abstract and transcultural terms, ignores cultural constraints on the individual, and offers only limited help in discussions of intercultural equality and fairness.

Equality before the law, equal protection of the law, and so on are also culturally mediated and call for cultural sensitivity. A law banning the use of drugs apparently treats all equally, but in fact it discriminates against those for whom some drugs are religious or cultural requirements, as in the case with Peyote and Marijuana respectively for the American Indians and the Rastafarians. This does not mean that the law may not ban their use, but rather that it should appreciate their unequal impact and have strong reasons for denying exemption to the two groups. The United States government showed the requisite cultural sensitivity when it exempted the ceremonial use of wine by Jews and Catholics during the prohibition period.

Prima facie the principle of equality requires that the law should be uniform in its application and content. However, situations do arise when it allows different treatment. Given the horrible nature of the Holocaust and the persistent streak of anti-semitism in its cultural life, it makes perfect sense for Germany to single out attacks on Jews for harsher punishment and to treat these as cases of aggravated assault. In a society in which specific cultural, ethnic or religious minorities have long been demonised and are frequent targets of discriminatory treatment, discrimination against them but not against others might be declared illegal or subjected to more severe penalties. At one level the differential treatment of these groups appears to confer a privilege on them; in fact it is only designed to equalise these especially vulnerable groups with the rest of the community.

In these and other cases we are concerned to ensure equality across cultures, and that is not easy. In a culturally homogenous society individuals share broadly similar needs, dispositions and desires. Since equal treatment here means a broadly identical treatment, the principle of equality is easy to apply, and discriminatory deviations from it are easy to identify. In a culturally diverse society, individual dispositions, needs, capacities, and so on vary considerably, and differences confront us at each stage. In order to treat such individuals equally, we need to identify and interpret these differences, distinguish those that are relevant, assess their comparative significance for the individuals concerned, and arrive at a form of treatment that is broadly equal. More often than not, equal treatment here will mean differential and not identical treatment, raising the question as to how we can ensure that the differential treatment is really equal and not a cloak for discrimination. Although there is no foolproof criterion of it, we should look at equality of effect (which is not the same as equality of outcome) rather than at the formal identity of rights. Our earlier discussions show what this implies.

Thanks to the centuries of discourse on equality in the context of a homogenous society, we have become so accustomed to equating equality with identical treatment, and differential treatment with inequality, that we feel intellectually disorientated in coping with culturally diverse societies. On the one hand, we appreciate that people are different in their needs and capacities, and that our treatment of them should take full account of this. On the other hand every form of differential treatment, especially of cultural minorities, arouses our deepest fears and anxieties, lest it should lead to an injustice or privilege. A good deal of our resistance to state support for minority languages and cultures and even to some form of affirmative action springs from this unease. If we are to ensure fairness and equality in culturally diverse societies, we need to do two things: first, we must appreciate that equal treatment might have to be different and not identical in its content, and second, we need to develop appropriate conceptual and institutional tools to ensure that different treatment does not lead to unfair discrimination or privilege.

A good society should aim to ensure equal treatment to all its citizens, including its cultural minorities. However well-intentioned and generous it might be, its capacity to do so is limited. First, it has a specific character or identity which it has acquired over the centuries and which is deeply woven into its way of life. It is therefore necessarily partial to a specific way of life and cannot treat all its constituent ways of life impartially. Although it can and should periodically redefine its identity to accommodate new needs and demands, it cannot do so beyond a certain point without losing its coherence and causing widespread disorientation and resentment. A society needs to be sensitive to both its past and its present, to the claims of both its majority and minorities, and to find ways of reconciling the demands of equality with the need to retain its sense of historical continuity. What sometimes gives multiculturalism a deservedly bad name is its tendency to undermine a society's identity and cultural coherence and to reduce it to a characterless collection of discrete groups in the name of giving a full equality of status to all its cultural communities within the framework of a culturally neutral and bland state.

Second, a culturally diverse society is characterised by a wide range of sometimes quite deep differences, all of them making all kinds of claims on it. However sensitive a society might be, its moral energies are limited, and it cannot be equally sensitive or sympathetic to all differences. It cannot be equally tolerant of them all either, nor willing to make the constant changes in its practices and beliefs that their accommodation requires. And since its understanding of different cultures is limited, its capacity to fine tune the principle of equality to their differences is also limited. All this means that no society can ever ensure full equality to all its cultural minorities. This does not at all mean that it should not constantly strive towards that goal, or that unjustly treated minorities should not put constant pressure on it, but rather that we should not take too harsh a view of its limitations and that its minorities should bear this fact in mind in formulating their demands.

Finally, although cultural equality is an important value, it is not the only one. Uniformity, efficiency, respect for the rights of others, collective interests of the organisation concerned, social harmony, a climate of trust and goodwill, and spontaneous co-operation of others are also important collective values, and demands for equality need to be balanced against them. Much of what makes human life valuable depends on the goodwill and spontaneous co-operation of others, and falls outside the ambit of claims and rights. A cultural minority that stridently insists on its rights in disregard of their cultural, organisational and other costs risks losing in the long run far more that what it gains in the short run. And so does a majority that brazenly takes advantage of its vulnerable and powerless minorities, and exaggerates its incapacity to make such changes in its way of life as are required by their legitimate demands and can be easily accommodated. The language of claims and counterclaims, insistence on one's due, and so forth, which are all inherent in the ultimately atomistic principle of equality, do have an important place in social life. But they must not be allowed to obscure the central fact that our lives overlap at countless points, that we are profoundly influenced by how others lead their lives, and that every society is ultimately sustained and indeed made bearable by the spirit of charity, good will, and mutual respect and accommodation.

Endnotes

1. Ahmad's case is described in detail in Sebastian Poulter (1980) *English Law and Ethnic Minority Customs*, London: Butterworths, pp. 247 ff.

2. For details, see Poulter, *op cit.*

3. Goldman v Weinberger 475 US 503 (1986).

4. Khalsa v. Weinberger, 787 F 2d. 1288, (1986).

5. Cited in Gloria T. Beckley and Paul Bernstein (1991) "Religious Pluralism, Equal Opportunity and the State", *The Western Political Quarterly*, Vol 44, p.202.

6. For details see Poulter, *op cit.*

7. For useful discussion, see Anna Elisabetta Galeotti (1993) "Citizenship and Equality: The Place for Toleration", *Political Theory*, Vol 21, pp. 585-605; and Norma Claire Moruzzi (1994) "A problem with head scarves; Contemporary Complexities of Political and Social Identity", *Political Theory*, Vol 22, pp 653-671.

8. See Tariq Modood (1992) *Not Easy Being British*, London: Trentham Books.

9. See Bhikhu Parekh (ed) (1990) *Law, Blasphemy and the Multi-Faith Society*, London: Commission for Racial Equality.

10. For a fuller philosophical discussion, see my "Cultural Diversity and Liberal Democracy," in David Beetham, (ed) (1994) *Defining and Measuring Democracy*, London: Sage.

The Attractions of Basic Income
Brian Barry

The starting point for this essay is a familiar story: the worldwide intellectual malaise of the political left. This is not necessarily incompatible with the electoral success of parties of the left but in office their performance seems increasingly indistinguishable from that of their rivals. Politicians are busy people for whom fifteen minutes thinking about one subject is a long time. With extremely rare exceptions, they do not originate ideas. Rather, they pick them up from others and adapt them to their own purposes. If politicians of the left are adrift, this is a reflection of the lack of a coherent alternative to the prevailing market-oriented ideology.

Out of the many statements of the problem that I have read, I choose for its comprehensiveness and succinctness that put forward by Henry Milner, whose diagnosis runs as follows:

> Despite the defeat of state socialism, people in the industrialised world have not been won over to rightist sensibilities. Eyewitness accounts in the media continually evoke the immortality of extreme inequality. The ideal – the enlightenment version of the good society as a community of free and equal people – is still very much alive. But we lack a theoretical framework through which we can convert our sensibilities and ideals into practical, real-world choices that decrease inequality. For all the writing and discussion, there is no distinguishable social-democratic or egalitarian political economy to replace the failed Marxist one, no systematic analysis of institutional arrangements in a society of free choice on the basis of their performance in producing and – fairly – distributing resources.[1]

Faced with the magnitude of the challenge outlined by Milner, it is tempting to withdraw from intellectual engagement with politics. (Such a response is not inconsistent with continuing to give time and money to whichever political party one regards as the least obnoxious.) This is a path trodden by many ex-Marxists who have rationalised their feelings of futility by embracing some variety of postmodern thought. The driving force here is the assumption that, if there is no single formula for social transformation (eg the total abolition of capitalism), there is nothing worth saying.

This passivity may be contrasted with an opposite reaction to what is in essence the same diagnosis: that between them economic and electoral constraints rule out anything except slight variations on the *status quo*. The alternative to intellectual passivity is intellectual hyperactivity: in the absence of any big idea, let there be an unlimited number of little ones. The upshot is a myriad of proposals for incremental improvements to existing institutions, each of which is argued for independently on its own merits. Such an approach is entirely honourable, and if the diagnosis is accurate, it is hard to see how anything better can be hoped for. It is as well, however, to be aware that this is scarcely a formula for the revitalisation of the left. Even if we are too disillusioned to be believe in a New Jerusalem, must the limits of our vision be confined to a slightly better-organised version of what we have now?

The result is, in any case, clear to see. As far as the vast majority of the population is concerned, politics is reduced to the positional manoeuvres of politicians, leaked internal party documents, politicians who stray from the party line, and similar trivia. Meanwhile, enthusiasts for the minutiae of policy, a few hundred people at the absolute outside – constantly reappear in different combinations to issue reports recommending the tweaking of welfare benefits and taxes, some slightly new managerial twist to the National Health Service, and so on. The same names and the same proposals come round and round again in commissions set up the Labour party, the Liberal Democrats or the Rowntree Trust, reports by organisations such as the Institute for Fiscal Studies and the Institute for Public Policy Research or, of all else fails, edited collections of essays by the same people and containing the same ideas. The point is, however, that all this frenetic activity has virtually no impact outside the circle of those engaged in it.

A case in point is the fate of the Report of the Commission on Social Justice.[2] This was set up amid a good deal of publicity by

John Smith, the then Leader of the Labour party, but when it eventually appeared its report utterly failed to capture the public imagination. Within a few weeks it was forgotten. No doubt the Commission was unlucky, as far as internal Labour party politics was concerned, by the unexpected death of its patron while it was still deliberating. But its very vulnerability to this kind of chance illustrates one of the reasons for its wider failure. As its members were prepared to say in private, they spent a good deal of time looking over their shoulders at the Labour leadership and tailored their recommendations with an eye to acceptability. This extremely narrow conception of the constraints of political feasibility inevitably made for an invertebrate document. It was perhaps inevitable that those who drafted the report were reduced to cobbling together proposals originating from the various pressure groups associated with different members of the Commission.

There were a lot of other things wrong with the Commission on Social Justice, beginning (as G A Cohen shows elsewhere in this book) with its highly dispiriting discussion of the concept of social justice. (I shall come back to this later.) But for the present purpose the most salient error was a fundamental misconception of the appropriate timescale. Instead of setting an agenda for a generation, what it produced looked more like a set of draft white papers for an incoming government. The lesson that has to be learned is the one provided by the success of the pro-market think tanks. They hammered away at their theme with scant regard for narrowly-conceived political feasibility. In this way they succeeded in creating an intellectual climate in which previously unthinkable ideas became thinkable and then in due course capable of being put into practice. Unless the counterparts of these pro-marketeers are willing to move away from their current short-termism, there is no chance of their seizing the political initiative.

My object in this essay is to present in brief compass the case for a single measure which would when fully implemented make a significant difference to the quality of many people's lives. The measure in question is an income paid unconditionally to all adults: a basic income or (as it is sometimes called) citizens' income. It is the lack of conditionality that marks a departure from any welfare state or social insurance system of the familiar kind. One way of looking at it is as an extension to adults of the principle of child benefit, which is an unconditional payment of precisely the kind envisaged.

Nothing is build into the definition of basic income about the level at which it must be pitched. Those who advocate the introduction of the measure normally assume that it will initially be set at a relatively low level, so that those with no other source of income would still need to have it supplemented by the usual welfare state benefits. However, many of the attractions of basic income come into play only when it reaches a level at which it is sufficient to live on. By the same token, the objections to basic income also have a far greater force if it is set at subsistence level than if it is below that level. (By "subsistence level" I mean the same as "enough to live on", putting on one side for the moment any controversy about how that is to be assessed.) Although there are real merits in even a low level of basic income (as I shall argue later), the most interesting and important questions concern the pros and cons of subsistence level basic income. I shall therefore focus on these, while accepting the common presupposition that any move to a system of subsistence level basic income would have to be phased in over a period to be measured in decades, rather than years.

I have mentioned in passing that basic income has its supporters. The idea has been rediscovered at intervals ever since Tom Paine put forward a version of it in the *Rights of Man*.[3] It is the policy of Green parties in Europe and has a Europe-wide organisation dedicated to its propagation, the Basic Income European Network. In Britain, the introduction of basic income is the policy of the Green party and was for several years the policy of the Liberal Democrats, though so little was made of it that few people seem to have noticed. There is also an organisation, Citizen's Income, which puts out a newsletter and research publications containing material favourable to basic income.

Despite all this, my own experience has been that, even among those with some interest in public policy issues, the very idea of basic income is unfamiliar. Why has such an essentially simple idea failed to make the breakthrough into mainstream political discourse? My conjecture is that too little effort has been expended on explaining the merits of the proposal and showing why apparently attractive alternatives are non-starters. Only after all that has been done is it appropriate to get into details about how precisely the transition to basic income might be staged, how it could be paid for, and so on. Instead of this, there is a great tendency in the literature to down play the radical potential of basic income and to treat as central to the proposal what is a technical by-product of it: the way in which it would streamline the benefit and tax system. It is quite true that as it stands this system – the word dignifies it too much – is a nightmare. Nobody believes that the sum of all the parts amounts to something admitting of rational justification. Nevertheless, it is important to emphasise that basic income is not just another idea for rejigging the existing system. Rather, it would be seen as offering a genuinely new deal – a different way of relating individual and society.

Another dominant feature in the advocacy of basic income is a tendency to get sucked prematurely into elaborate computations. This is quite enough to choke off interest among all except the most dedicated of policy buffs. It is, moreover, out of place. For no tax and benefit simulation, however conscientiously carried out, can make allowance for the changes in behaviour that would arise under an altered regime. A subsistence-level basic income would face people with an entirely different set of opportunities and incentives from those facing them now. We can speculate about the way in which they might respond, but it would be irresponsible to pretend that by cranking a lot of numbers through a computer we can turn any of that into hard science.

The underlying arithmetic of basic income is extremely simple, and it is worth understanding it. Let us take "subsistence" to mean not merely enough to keep body and soul together but enough to be an active participant in one's society, not debarred by poverty from playing a full part in its social, political and economic institutions. A variety of approaches (including opinion surveys) have converged on the notion that subsistence so defined requires an income half that of the average in one's society. Let us take this as our criterion of subsistence. Then, if the basic income is to provide everyone with this amount, it must take one quarter of the national income to supply it. How can this be paid for? The answer is: in any number of ways. But a straightforward and perspicuous way of thinking about it is to imagine a twenty-five per cent tax rate on all income. This would yield a sum equivalent to one quarter of the national income and thus balance the books. The rate required would be higher if some income were exempt (eg tax relief for private and occupational pensions and mortgage interest) but proponents of basic income normally assume these should go, as I do.

We would still be left with the need to raise money to support all other expenses of government, central and local, such as defence, police, education and health. In round figures, let us suppose that to pay for these services income would be taxed at fifty per cent and the rest raised by other taxes – including, perhaps, some innovative taxes on anti-social activities such as travel by air or private car, pollution, and currency and stock market speculation. This is as far as simple arithmetic can take us. What it leaves open is the level of national income at which the economy would settle with these arrangements and therefore the absolute level of the basic income.

On a very pessimistic projection, the availability of any unconditional income would result in such a catastrophic decline in the national income that the economy would reach equilibrium only at a point where the basic income was insufficient to keep body and soul together. An optimistic projection would emphasise in contrast the way in which the availability of an unconditional income would enable people to price themselves into jobs, so that the overall level of productive activity would be a good deal higher than in a welfare state system. This is where we cannot get away from speculation about the behavioural consequences of a major change in the structure of opportunities and incentives.

I believe that it is possible to show why the optimistic scenario is plausible. But it would be absurd to be dogmatic. What can be said is that it would be easy to gain better evidence once basic income was introduced at a low level and gradually raised. If the pessimists turned out to be right, there would be two options open. One would be to leave the income unconditional, but hold its level below the point at which it started to become attractive (or perhaps even physically possible) to live on it. The other would be to switch to a closely related idea that has been put forward under the name of "participation income" under which the prospect of a life of pure self-indulgence on a subsistence-level would be ruled out by requiring recipients to make a contribution of some kind or be ready to take paid employment. (I shall discuss this later, but even the present sketch would be incomplete without its mention).

Since I have been so bold as to talk openly about a flat tax on all income of fifty per cent (which would, of course, be made higher on larger incomes), it will perhaps be clear now why I emphasised the importance of not allowing one's thinking to be stultified by short-termism. At this stage, there are two things that need to be said. The first is to repeat that any move towards a subsistence-level basic income would inevitably be spread over a period measured in decades. If basic income at lower levels became popular, the taxes to pay for its extension would presumably be acceptable. The other point to be made is that there is something fundamentally irrational about the way in which tax rates are currently thought about. What is required is a change of *Gestalt*, and one way of helping to bring it about is to focus people's minds on the mechanics of basic income.

What I mean buy this is that fifty per cent tax rate is thought of as a lot, yet about one third of the British population rely on means-tested benefits of one sort or another (income support, family credit, housing benefit, and so on). Because of the way in which these benefits work together, and because in addition it is quite possible to pay income tax while at the same time drawing a means-tested benefit, the marginal tax rates that people on these benefits face run from seventy per cent up to one hundred per cent. Thus, earning more brings in little or no additional income unless earnings are so high as to break free of means-tested benefits altogether.

There are, I believe, reasons concerned with both equity and incentive for being far more worried about high marginal tax rates on low earnings than high ones. Somebody earning £3 per hour who faces an eighty per cent tax rate finishes up with 60p an hour; somebody earning £30 per hour still gets £6 per hour, which is not negligible. The only basis on which anybody can get exercised about high marginal tax rates in the second case but not in the first is by making everything turn on the withdrawal rate of a benefit as against the rate of imposition of tax. Yet it seems inconceivable that the same considerations of equity and incentive should not apply to both.

I have expressed the hope that the introduction of a basic income would facilitate the breaking down of this irrational compartmentalisation. My reason for being hopeful is quite simply this. Within the framework that makes a distinction between taxes and benefits, a basic income must count as a benefit. But then the tax that reduces its net value as income increases should be seen as the rate of withdrawal of a benefit and compared with the withdrawal rates of means-tested benefits. Of course, at a certain point the net value of the basic income is reduced to zero. (With a fifty per cent tax rate this occurs when other income is exactly double the level of the basic income.) At that point, then, we are presumably to think in terms of a tax rate rather than a benefit withdrawal rate. But surely it would be very hard under these conditions to attach any great significance to the difference.

With any luck it would become apparent that the only effect of moving up the income scale was that it would be less and less burdensome as income rose to pay a higher rate of tax. Perhaps it would after a long time become a source of wonderment that people had for so long put up with a system in which those with the lowest incomes faced exceedingly high marginal tax rates, those in the middle, the lowest marginal tax rates, and those in the top few per cent of the income distribution a somewhat higher rate but still only half or less than faced by most of those at the bottom.

Is basic income a Big Idea? If we require of a Big Idea that it should be a panacea, then it is not. But on that exacting criterion there are no Big Ideas. The archetypal Big Idea for the left is, as I have already said, the complete abolition of capitalism. But that would contribute nothing to questions about the organisation of the national health service or the educational system and would have little direct impact on housing policy or transport policy. Moreover, as the sad examples of the Soviet Union and China illustrate, there is nothing in the abolition of capitalism that makes for an enlightened approach to environmental questions. Among the many issues that would still be left open is the advisability of introducing a basic income, which might then take the rather attractive form of a dividend on the nation's capital.

Thus, basic income would still leave the policy buffs with plenty to do. Yet at the same time it would be unwise to underestimate the significance of replacing the existing mess of conditional benefits and grants with an unconditional income set at a level that would enable to live on it. The profoundest socialist thinkers have recognised that social equality is not only a matter of limited disparities in income but also turns on giving each person the dignity that comes from independence. Dependency – the dependency of a worker on an employer or a woman on a man – has rightly been seen as the enemy to be overcome. I do not think it too fanciful to claim that those who learned their socialism from William Morris and R H Tawney may recognise the introduction of a subsistence-level basic income as a practical way of achieving some of their central aims. Indeed, if we can manage to strip away the appalling legacy of "really existing socialism" and go back to Marx's original utopian vision, it is not absurd to suggest that a subsistence-level basic income is a far more plausible institutional embodiment of it than anything Marx himself ever came up with.

I have said that we should not expect any single measure – whether it be the abolition of capitalism or the introduction of a basic income – to provide a solution to all the questions that public policy analysts worry about. But is it worth pointing out, nevertheless, that many of them would be ameliorated if a subsistence-level basic income were in place. Thus, for example, the whole question of maintenance grants for those wishing to pursue post-secondary education would be automatically taken care of, since anyone prepared to live on the basic income would have the opportunity of using it to support them while studying, whether they choose as their field of study conventional academic subjects or those currently funded on a hit and miss basis (increasingly miss) such as acting, ballet or art. This would still leave the funding of tuition fees to be settled. Undoubtedly, there are good arguments from equity in favour of having tuition fees repaid over a period by the beneficiaries, and there are a variety of perfectly practical schemes that could be set up to achieve this. But it is worth stressing that, by removing the cost of maintenance from the equation, a basic income would obviously make the task of supporting the cost of higher education much more manageable.

Again, let us suppose that, over a time-span measured in decades like that appropriate to basic income, the main thrust of a sensible transport policy would be to phase out the private car and make the train the norm for long trips. This would clearly require public subsidy and control of a kind hitherto unknown in Britain (regardless of ownership) so as to make the railways the servants of the wider public interest. If people are to give up cars altogether, public transport has to run on regular schedules from early in the morning until late at night, as it does in many places on the continent of Europe already. Moreover, stations need to be manned during all the hours during which trains stop at them, to avoid the bleakness and sense of insecurity generated by empty platforms. I do not think it is a mere hangover of steam-age romanticism to suppose that the job of station master or assistant station master to a small station could be made to appeal to enough people to mean that it would be unnecessary to pay a lot to fill them. Within a regime that gave everybody enough to live on to begin with, even low earnings would make for a net addition to income and provide a margin above subsistence level. A job that was manifestly worthwhile, and seen by everybody as such, might well get takers at rates of pay that nobody under the current dispensation could afford to accept.

Jobs of this nature would suit the kinds of people who are among the most likely to be permanently unemployed at present: those over the age of forty with a limited amount of education. There are other jobs in which reliability rather than either brilliance or physical strength are similarly at a premium. Little imagination is required to think of ways in which the amenity of life could be enhanced by the creation of jobs that might prove sufficiently attractive to require only a relatively small supplement to the basic income to fill them. (Bear in mind that it is not necessary for a job to appeal to all those capable of doing it – only as many as are needed to fill the vacancies.) Voices are raised, very properly, about the amount of vandalism and unchecked anti-social behaviour that goes on in public parks. This would be dealt with by the recruitment of an adequate corps of park-keepers. Again, such jobs might well require little material reward to make them preferable to spending the day doing nothing. The same may be said of wardens in the countryside.

These are enough examples to make the point. Under a basic income system those running labour-intensive institutions such as schools and hospitals would be faced with an enormous incentive to design jobs that were congenial enough to encourage those with mediocre formal qualifications to take them at more of less nominal pay rates. Part-time work might well prove especially attractive, and would not run into any of the difficulties thrown up by the existing benefit system. It is not necessary to second guess the details to see the potential for the revamping of work that is offered by basic income.

It is, admittedly, possible to discern among the policy buffs and the politicians a dim recognition of the craziness of the present system, in which the unemployed are faced with a choice of idleness or criminality. If they want to retain their benefits, while hundreds of thousands of jobs that cry out to be filled do not exist because it would not be profitable to pay those doing them enough to make them better off than they are unemployed. Periodically the proposal surfaces that, instead of paying people to be idle, it might be sensible to pay the equivalent amount to employers in return for creating new jobs. But these proposals envisage only a short-term subsidy (say six months), and are thought of as only small-scale interventions. They might do something to churn the pool of long-term unemployed. But they would do very little to achieve the objective of reducing involuntary unemployment to a purely local phenomenon. (The Swedes, whose "active labour market policy" includes job subsidies, have recognised that the device is one that works well only if the unemployment rate is in any case running at only two or three per cent.) The point of scrapping the whole apparatus of conditional benefits and replacing it with basic income is that the money underwriting low-paid jobs is then permanent, automatic and universal; yet at the same time nobody is forced to take a job if none is attractive enough. Provided the basic income is genuinely adequate, we can then say that nobody is exploited, however low the pay. For the job is freely chosen in preference to an acceptable alternative of not having a job.

Let me conclude on a more speculative note, with a brief exploration of basic income and market socialism. Once we leave behind the band of initiates who staff the think-tanks, make up the commissions, and keep the conventional wisdom of the centre-left in circulation, we are hard put to it to find anything except these two ideas. It is therefore natural to wonder about their relation: are they in competition with one another, are they mutually supportive, or what?

An initial problem facing any such inquiry is that the term "market socialism" is used to refer to an enormous range of imagined economic systems. Perhaps the only feature that unites all self-styled market socialists is that they do not look for coordination between firms to be carried out by a central planning bureau with the power to allocate materials and labour or set prices. In place of this kind of imperative coordination, they anticipate that markets will carry the main burden. Out of the various possibilities, more or less far reaching in scope, I want to focus on one relatively modest form of market socialism that seems to me to bring with it certain characteristic attractions and drawbacks in an instructive way. Although it is doubtful that there is any interesting sense in which it is socialist, it does nevertheless make some connection with the ethos of guild socialism, which I take to have had its ethical roots in a concern for the collective autonomy of workers and an end to "wage slavery". Let us extract from this two ideas: first that those who work for a firm run it, according to some system of governance chosen by themselves; and, second, that wages and salaries are replaced by payments (not necessarily equal) that divide up what is left after meeting expenses and setting aside whatever amount is agreed on for investment.

Let me stipulate, in order to give the discussion some determinacy, that a state bank is set up with the mission of lending money to groups of workers who want to by out some existing firm or start a new one and manage it co-operatively. (It would be reasonable to set a limit of a few hundred workers, at least until experience with forms of governance had been gained.) The bank would, of course, be expected to back only what appeared to be sound prospects, and I assume that it would demand a realistic rate of return on its loans. In fact, all that would differentiate it from an ordinary commercial bank is that it would be less risk-averse, more closely involved in monitoring and advising the firm, and more committed for the long term. (Even those features would distinguish the model bank from a British commercial bank more than they would distinguish it from a German or Japanese bank.) The appeal of such a scheme is apparent, and I believe that it would be well worth creating a bank along those lines, even if it were funded initially with only a few hundred million points. It would hold the promise to the participants of combining liberation and personal responsibility in a way that the standard employment contract does not lend itself to. If it succeeded, its example would exert a beneficial pressure on conventionally organised firms to offer a better deal to their own workers. And, from a purely instrumental point of view, it would be a way of introducing flexibility into the economy while averting the usual counterpart of flexibility, exploitation.

However, if any such scheme were introduced against the background of the existing tax and benefit system it would run into two snags. The first is that a new firm (or an old one, especially if it had been bought out to forestall its closure) might well take many months before it could cover more than payments to its suppliers and the bank. The workers would not be eligible for welfare state benefits because they would not meet the criterion of being available for work, so the only way of carrying on would be to add the cost of paying the workers to the firm's debt. This would be a daunting prospect and might well discourage most potentially viable co-operatives from getting started.

The second snag is that firms run in the way described here would be a potent source of income inequality. It is true that within-firm disparities would probably be less wide than would the gap between employees in similar jobs in conventional firms: both sociological theory and such experience as there is of workers' co-operatives support this prediction. But there would inevitably be a very large variance in the profitability of different firms. This would feed through directly into large differences between the payments made to people doing similar jobs, depending on the success of their firm. Clearly, one has to accept that, if the "market" element in market socialism is to work, there must be rewards for success. But surely the "socialism" should at the very least mean that the scale of these rewards should be tempered by the demands of solidarity, and the current tax system has little to contribute to that.

I can now return to the question with which I began this discussion of market socialism: what is its relation to basic income? My suggestion is that basic income would facilitate market socialism by taking care of the two snags just outlined. Thus, let us suppose that a subsistence-level basic income was already present by the time a scheme for lending money to workers' co-operatives was introduced. The bank might make it a test of the serious intent of applicants for funding that they should not seek to borrow money to pay themselves but should be prepared to live on the basic income until the firm was profitable enough to pay them. This would usefully sort out those for whom forming part of a workers' co-operative was genuinely valuable from those with no such commitment. But for those who were prepared to go ahead on these terms, it would keep the burden of debt down and thus remove a major deterrent from forming a co-operative in the first place. From the side of the bank, it would have the great advantage of limiting its exposure to any particular co-operative and enabling it to make any given allocation of funding go further.

As far as the second snag is concerned, the system of a basic income at subsistence level and the associated taxes to pay for it might be regarded as a tolerable solution. Let us suppose that a co-operative was able to cover its outgoings and provide its workers with a life they found worthwhile, but did not have enough left over to pay them very much. Then they would have the basic income to add to the (post-tax) income they received from the firm. Conversely, if the firm were lucky enough to make a lot of money for its workers, an equitable system of income tax would ensure that their good fortune was shared with others. I am not to be taken as suggesting that, if there was nothing else to be said for basic income, it would be worth introducing it simply in order to make market socialism work better. If I am right, however, there are many other reasons for supporting basic income, it can then be regarded as a plus that it would make an experiment with market socialism more likely to succeed.

I make no pretence of having done more in this essay than explore a very few of the ramifications of basic income. I could have talked about its transformative potential for the voluntary sector and its role in relation to care for children and elderly or infirm relatives. I could have explored the reasons for the affinity between green politics and basic income, and discussed the possibilities of basic income as a vehicle of transfers from rich countries to poor ones. My objective here has been a modest one: to suggest that the idea of basic income is worth taking seriously as a way forward for the left.

Endnotes

1. Henry Milner (1994) *Social Democracy and Rational Choice: The Scandinavian Experience and Beyond*, London: Routledge, p4.

2. *Social Justice: Strategies for National Renewal*, London: Vintage (1994).

3. T Paine *Rights of Man* H Collins (ed) (1969), Harmondsworth: Penguin.